ACKNOWLEDGMENTS

I would like to thank Dr. Charles Kibert for his assistance and guidance on this research project. To Dr. Gary Koehler I am grateful for both his technical input and his guidance in course selections in the decision and information sciences. I would also like to thank Drs. Weilin Chang and Carleton Coulter for their concern and academic guidance.

I want to express my deepest gratitude to Dianne Woodbury, for without her editorial skills this dissertation would not have been possible. To my wife, Gail, credit is due for her typing assistance and for putting up with me during this difficult process.

TABLE OF CONTENTS

APPENDICES

LIST OF FIGURES

Abstract of Dissertation Presented to the Graduate School
of the University of Florida in Partial Fulfillment of the
Requirements for the Degree of Doctor of Philosophy

AN EXTENDED STRUCTURED QUERY LANGUAGE
INCORPORATING OBJECT DATA TYPES
FOR THE
CONSTRUCTION INDUSTRY

By

Kevin C. Hollister

August 1992

Chairman: Weilin P. Chang, Ph.D.
Major Department: Architecture

The purpose of this research is to extend the relational query language SQL

to provide construction industry-specific functions to aid in the retrieval of

construction information. The first chapter of this dissertation introduces its

organization and purpose. Chapter 2 provides both the history and background of

SQL, which serve as the foundations for the construction-specific SQL extensions.

To provide a clear understanding of the basic principles and structure of SQL, a

review of its primary functions and syntax is presented in Chapter 3. SQL's relational

operators, and its keys and keywords provided the basis for further development in

Chapter 4. Although previous extensions to SQL have been undertaken, none has

addressed the unique needs and vernacular of the construction industry. Chapter 4

focuses on these distinct requirements and discusses the use of object data typing,

object attributes, and user-defined functions as they relate to the Construction

Industry-SQL (CI-SQL) extensions. In Chapter 5, two primary applications are examined. In the construction materials domain, five extensions are created that directly address the selection of materials during the design and bidding phases of the construction process. In the second domain, construction scheduling, an additional five extensions are developed that are applicable to the retrieval of scheduling information. The provision of a model for the evolution of construction industry-specific SQL extensions in these two domains, has advanced the application of computers for managing construction information. The final chapter, Chapter 6, describes the conclusions of this research and addresses the need for future research in this area.

CHAPTER 1
INTRODUCTION

While the 1980's will be remembered as the era of the microcomputer revolution, the 1990's are shaping up as the age of the data base explosion. The battle for the desktop has been won. Microcomputers are more powerful than ever, and the increased processing power is being used for applications traditionally reserved for minicomputers and mainframes, like data base management. The desktop has become a window to access corporate information. (Crutchfield, 1990, p. 193)

In few industries is accessing information more crucial than in the construction industry. Issues such as retrieving detailed information on the availability and cost of construction materials, as well as determining the interrelationships among project activities, are critical components in providing the construction industry with the information services it requires. By providing such services productivity increases can be realized through improved methods of information retrieval. These improvements are primarily derived from the addition of industry-specific vocabulary. At a macroscopic level the addition of vocabulary with which construction professionals are already familiar begins to tailor an application to the specific information needs of the construction industry. With multiple key players (e.g., the owner, the architect, and the contractor) timely and accurate information sharing is a vital ingredient to a successful project. The difficulty in sharing this information is exacerbated by project participants who may be in different geographical locations and may be using incompatible computer systems. Presently, no solution has been developed for these problems inherent to the construction industry.

1

Concurrent with the business world's acceptance of relational data base management systems (RDBMSs) as the preferred method of managing business data, Structured Query Language (SQL) has become the de facto standard for accessing this data. While SQL may be adequate for industries that do not have a specialized vocabulary, it falls short of meeting the information needs of the construction industry. It is the purpose of this dissertation, therefore, to extend SQL to address the unique information demands of the construction enterprise. This SQL extension will be referred to as Construction Industry SQL (CI-SQL). This dissertation will be organized as follows.

1.1 Dissertation Organization

Chapter 2 will be a review of the history of the relational data base and the development of structured query language. This historical analysis will include the relational model developed by E.F. Codd from which relational data bases were derived. Significant events that shaped SQL and eventually caused it to become a standard will also be discussed. Additionally, current problems in the standardization process as well as measures being undertaken to resolve these dilemmas will be included to further explain the current status of SQL in industry use. A discussion of these events and issues will help familiarize the reader with significant developments and provide a theoretical framework for the applied extension of SQL.

In Chapter 3 an overview of the relational model and SQL will be presented. The structure of SQL, including its syntax and semantics, will be explained in sufficient detail to provide an adequate, but by no means comprehensive, description of the mechanics of the language. Additionally, relational operators, keys, and key words will be included to highlight the features of SQL. Query examples will be given to provide the framework for construction-specific queries. Thus, this chapter will supply a foundation for the extension of SQL in the subsequent chapter.

In Chapter 4 the guidelines used for extending SQL to meet construction needs will be explained. Since the author's purpose is not to improve SQL but rather to provide an industry-specific extension to the language, the SQL standard, as accepted by the American National Standard Institute and its X3 Committee, will be left unchanged. The design methodology used in arriving at a "superset" of SQL will be detailed.

In Chapter 5 the new construction-specific vocabulary of the Construction Industry-SQL, CI-SQL, will be generated and explained. From this vocabulary the new command syntax will be derived and explained. The product of this chapter will provide the construction industry with additional tools beneficial in managing an industry-specific relational data base.

The final chapter, Chapter 6, will summarize the findings of the research project and discuss specific areas of the language that necessitate further investigation. Consequently, the author acknowledges that this research and product are not the completion of a process but rather the fundamental basis for providing the construction industry with extensions to a query language designed to meet its specific needs.

1.2 Dissertation Purpose

The essence of these chapters will serve to generate new knowledge in several specific areas. First, the concept of an industry-specific SQL will be developed to include an industry with some of the most extensive information needs of any business. Secondly, guidelines for extending SQL to assist in the management of construction information systems will be set forth. Finally, the language of SQL will be extended to include a construction vocabulary and command syntax that will provide the construction industry with a several query capabilities tailored to meet its specific informational needs.

While CI-SQL can play a significant role in changing the way information is retrieved by the construction industry, it is in no way a complete solution to the many problems of managing construction information. In order to provide a comprehensive solution to information management, several issues must be resolved. Initially, robust construction data bases must be developed that support SQL. This support should be unquestionably provided since SQL is the de facto standard for relational query languages. Second, the author does not assume that construction professionals would become data-base professionals as well. To maximize the user's ability to utilize the extensions described in this work, a customized user interface would have to be developed that would provide storage and easy access to repetitive commands. This interface might well be developed under a graphical user interface such as Microsoft Windows or IBM's OS/2. Such an interface could further simplify the process of building and repeating queries. A less tangible, but no less important, issue to be resolved is that of industry acceptance. Such acceptance would require a complete rethinking of the way the construction industry currently accesses information. Since the construction industry has a distinct reputation for resisting change the difficulty of this task should not be underestimated. Finally, the implementation of many of the ideas described in this research would mandate a resolve on the part of the industry to minimize the enormous duplication of work that currently exists in the design and construction processes. Much of the information pertaining to materials and their associated costs and availability must first be obtained by the project designers and then again by all companies bidding on the project. This duplication of effort could be greatly limited by passing this information along in electronic form from the design team to the construction team. CI-SQL could aid in this process by furnishing an industry-specific vocabulary of data base operators that could be used by anyone familiar with construction terminology. Based on these issues it should be apparent that CI-SQL is just one of several important ingredients in the overall solution to the informational requirements of the construction industry.

1.3 Summary

In addition to generating new knowledge, this research will augment the existing body of knowledge in two key ways. First, the information requirements of the construction industry will be more adequately met by applying existing management information system techniques to construction. Secondly, additional evidence advocating the adoption of an application independent SQL standard will be presented. Through these contributions, progress can be made toward advancing the state-of-the-art in managing design and construction information.

CHAPTER 2
HISTORY AND BACKGROUND OF SQL

This chapter will provide readers with ample history and the background information necessary to grasp the fundamental principles of relational data bases and their companion query language, SQL. Beginning with E.F. Codd's relational model, an explanation of the concepts and terminology of relational data bases will be presented. It was in response to this foundational work that SQL began to emerge as the preeminent tool for accessing relational data. As it developed, several significant events transpired that forged a direction and determined the structure of SQL. Due to its sound theoretical basis and its solid practical application, SQL was accepted and designated as an international standard. The process of becoming a standard, however, is not without its pitfalls. Its proponents and critics have debated the merits and faults of the SQL standard in a continuing effort to refine its attributes and applications. Therefore, the life of the Structured Query Language, from its inception through its current state, will be discussed.

2.1 Data Base Concepts

The concept of a data base is a rather simple one. It is merely a collection of data. Construction professionals deal with loosely defined data bases daily in the form of employee files, historical estimating data, and even weekly timesheets. Although these collections of data may not appear to be data bases, in a simplistic sense they clearly meet the definition of a data base. At a more formal level "a data

6

base is a shared collection of interrelated data designed to meet the varied information needs of an organization" (McFadden & Hoffer, 1988, p. 3). One particular type of data base, the relational data base, and its associated query language, will be the basis of this research. In its simplest form a relational data base is a collection of two-dimensional tables. A table is composed of rows and columns whose intersections are often called fields. Each row in a table is frequently referred to as a record which is a single, usually unique, instance of data. For example, an employee data base could contain the last name, first name, age and employee number of all current employees. The relational model, detailed in the subsequent section, gained tremendous popularity in the 1970's over other models for two fundamental reasons. First, the simple approach of organizing data in tables was appealing to data base developers as well as users. Second, the relational system supports access by the end user rather than just the system programmer. This accessibility opened the door for the creation of ad hoc queries that allowed the user to retrieve data in almost any desired format. These characteristics of relational data bases blend well with the varied information retrieval needs of the construction industry.

2.2 Origin of Relational Data Bases

In 1970, while working at IBM's Research Laboratory in San Jose, California, E.F. Codd published his definitive paper, "A Relational Model of Data for Large Shared Data Banks" (Codd, 1970). The technology for the entire domain of relational data bases emanated from this foundational work. In this paper, Codd "laid down a set of abstract principles for data base management: the so-called *relational model*" (Date, 1989, p. 1). According to Pascal (1989b), "His relational model, based on the set mathematics of relations of first-order predicate logic, covers the three aspects of data that any DBMS must address: structure, integrity, and manipulation" (p. 248). These characteristics were originally set forth in the form of a set of features as follows:

A. Structural features
R-Tables
Base (stored)
View (virtual)
Query (derived)
Snapshot

Domains

Columns

Keys
Primary (PK)
Foreign (FK)

B. Integrity features
Entity integrity
Referential integrity
Domain integrity
Column integrity
User-defined integrity

C. Manipulative features
Basic operations
Assignment
Project
Restrict
Product
Union
Difference

Derived operations
Join
Intersect
Divide

Extended operations
Outer
Maybe
Domain override

2.3 Codd's Twelve Fidelity Rules

Due to misunderstandings and distortions, Codd later created his now famous Twelve Fidelity Rules, a minimum of six of which must be met in order for a data base management system to be considered truly relational. Although this set of rules is titled The Twelve Fidelity Rules, Codd intentionally began with Rule 0 which serves as a mandatory foundation for all relational DBMSs. These rules, as outlined by Pascal in "A Brave New World" (Pascal, 1989b, p. 249) are given as follows:

Rule 0: Foundation Rule

Any system that is advertised as, or claimed to be, a relational DBMS, must manage the data base entirely through its relational capabilities.

Rule 1: Information Rule

All information in a relational data base must be represented explicitly at the logical level in exactly one way by table values.

Rule 2: Guaranteed Access Rule

Each and every data value in a relational data base is guaranteed to be logically accessible by resorting to a combination of table name, column name, and primary key value.

Rule 3: Missing Information Rule

Missing value indicators distinct from empty character strings, strings of blank characters, zero, or any other numbers, must represent and support, in operations at the logical level in a systematic way independent of data type, the fact that values are missing for applicable and inapplicable information.

Rule 4: System Catalog Rule

The description of the data base is represented at the logical level dynamically like ordinary data so that authorized users can apply the same (relational) language to its interrogation.

Rule 5: Comprehensive Language Rule

No matter how many languages and terminal interactive modes are supported, at least one language must be supported that is expressible as character strings per some well-defined syntax that supports interactively by program
  1 - data definition
  2 - integrity constraints
  3 - data manipulation
  4 - views
  5 - transaction boundaries
  6 - authorization privileges

Rule 6: View Updatability Rule

The DBMS must have a way of determining at view definition time whether a view can be used to insert rows, delete rows, or update which columns of its underlying base tables and store the results in the system catalog.

Rule 7: Set Level Updates Rule

The capability of operating on whole tables applies not only to retrieval but also to insertion, modification, and deletion of data.

Rule 8: Physical Data Independence Rule

Application programs and interactive operations should not have to be modified whenever changes are made in internal storage or access methods.

Rule 9: Logical Data Independence Rule

Application programs and interactive operations should not have to be modified whenever certain types of changes involving no loss of information are made to the base tables.

Rule 10: Integrity Independence Rule

Application programs and interactive operations should not have to be modified whenever changes are made in integrity constraints defined by the data language and stored in the catalog.

Rule 11: Distribution Independence Rule

Application programs and interactive operations should not have to be modified whenever data is distributed or redistributed on different computers.

Rule 12: Nonsubversion Rule

If a DBMS has a low-level (procedural) language, that language should not be allowed to subvert or bypass integrity constraints or security constraints expressed in the high level relational level.

2.4 Origin and Implementation of Structured Query Language

As with any data base system, facilities must be provided for retrieving information from the data base. The language used to perform these retrievals is called a query language. "When E.F. Codd introduced the concept of a relational data base in 1970, he suggested that, 'the adoption of a relational model of data . . . permits the development of a universal data sublanguage based on an applied predicate calculus.' Although he indicated the requirements and the advantages of such a language, he did not attempt at that time to devise one" (Hursch & Hursch, 1988, p. 1). However, in 1974 D.D. Chamberlin and R.F. Boyce published their work, "SEQUEL: A Structured English Query Language," which presented the structure and format of a relational data base query language (Hursch & Hursch,

1988, p. 1). In his book, <u>A Guide to the SQL Standard</u> (1989), C.J. Date details the evolution of SQL products based upon Chamberlin and Boyce's work.

The initial implementation of a standard query language was in the IBM relational prototype, SEQUEL - XRM. This product was subsequently revised and released under the name SEQUEL/2. For legal reasons, this product's name was later changed to SQL. Thereafter, IBM implemented SEQUEL/2 in its research data base, System R. During the lifetime of the System R project, several modifications were made to the syntax of SQL including the addition of an EXISTS function and outer joins. Due to the success of System R, IBM began working on additional commercial SQL products. In an effort to compete with IBM, other vendors, such as Relational Software, began developing their own SQL products. Relational's release of its product, ORACLE, actually predated the market entry of IBM's SQL product, SQL/DS. SQL/DS, designed for the DOS VSE environment, was quickly followed by a VM/CMS version in 1982. DB2, an MVS product compatible with SQL/DS, was released in 1983. In the years that followed, various vendors entered the arena with SQL-based products including Hewlett-Packard, Sybase, Gupta Technologies, Digital Equipment, Teradata, Ingres, and Informix. With a myriad of vendors producing SQL products an inevitable variety of SQL dialects ensued. In response to this proliferation, the American National Standards Institute (ANSI) created its Data Base Committee, X3H2. This committee, composed of vendors and users, began to attempt to set standards for the SQL language in 1982. Simultaneously, the International Standards Organization's Remote Data Access committee, ISO/RDA, has been working on a standard client/server interface for multiple computing platforms.

2.5 Standardization of SQL

The SQL standard, "which was finally ratified by ANSI in 1986, consisted essentially of the IBM dialect of SQL," including its many idiosyncrasies (Date, 1989, p. 3). The following year the ISO/RDA accepted ANSI's work as an international standard. It is this standard, ANSI/SQL level 1, which is usually referred to as "the SQL standard." It is also the "only concrete expression of the relational model that has gained industry acceptance" (Pascal, 1989b, p. 250). "Since 1987, both the ANSI and ISO committees have been meeting and refining their standardization efforts. ANSI/SQL level 2 should be published in 1992; the RDA work will not be completed until 1992" (Crutchfield, 1990, p. 194). In addition to the quasi-governmental standards organizations, several industry driven consortiums have been working on developing their own standards. These groups include the X/Open Consortium and the SQL Access Group (Crutchfield, 1990, p. 194). The emergence of these industry associations has primarily been a response to the ever-changing needs of users in the marketplace. The development of these SQL standards organizations is summarized in Figure 1 (Crutchfield, 1990, p. 194).

The fact that SQL is a language designed for accessing relational data bases rather than a complete application development language has assisted in three primary ways in its acceptance as a standard. First, the well-defined, set-oriented data base foundation can be delineated from the more loosely defined, procedural nature of existing programming languages. Secondly, the pitfalls of developing

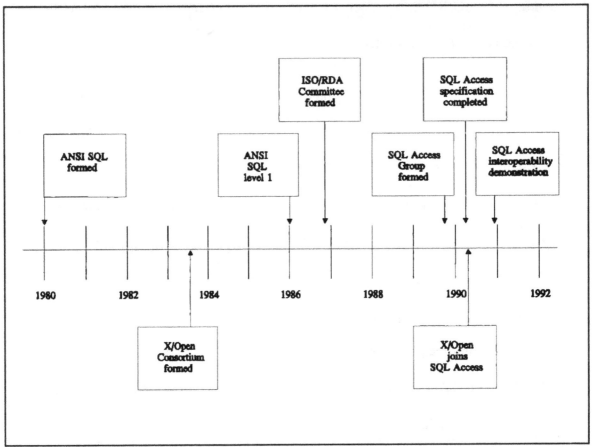

Figure 1 The Standards Organizations

another general purpose language, such as complexity and attempts to create

aprogramming panacea, can be avoided. Thirdly, the difficult political process of

extending mainstream procedural languages to address relational data base

requirements can be averted (Pascal, 1989b, p. 250). The actual process of selecting

a model for the standard, however, was somewhat arbitrary. The chairman of the

committee developing the structured query language standard in the United States,

Don Deutsch, remembers, "We just chose from between the existing products to

establish a least common denominator standard" (Moad, 1990, p. 27). Clearly, the

standardization of SQL is an evolving process and one that is not without problems.

2.6 Weaknesses of SQL

For anything to become a standard, it must inevitably encounter numerous difficulties; SQL is no exception to this rule. One of the most difficult obstacles for SQL to overcome is for it to be capable of communicating across multiple hardware and software platforms. Since a typical relational data base management system (RDBMS) installation may include hardware and software supplied by several different vendors, this problem is nontrivial. Although many vendors have attempted to resolve this situation through various forms of interfaces and integration, complete interoperability has not yet been achieved.

The above problem is compounded when one considers the numerous dialects of SQL that currently exist in the marketplace. This prevents one vendor's SQL product from accessing the data in other SQL products. This problem is magnified by the sheer number of SQL programs. "According to industry estimates, there are more than 140 implementations of SQL RDBMSes in use" (Crutchfield, 1990, p. 196). Initially this problem may seem somewhat trivial; however, consider the following practical example: An individual may have a checking account, a credit card, overdraft protection, and a loan all at the same bank. Pertinent information for all of these bank services could be contained in different data bases. If a bank's customers were to move and submit a change of address, it is very likely that all the records would have to be updated individually since each bank service's information probably resides on a different heterogeneous data base (Crutchfield, 1990, p. 196).

The problem of intercommunication is complicated by each vendor's use of various communication protocols. This prevents the connection to and communication between competing SQL products. Just as users strongly desire the ability to import and export between similar software applications, they are also requesting the ability to communicate with different RDBMSs on multiple computing platforms.

Technology also poses its own unique set of difficulties for the standardization process. Rapidly changing technology makes it extremely difficult for standards committees to keep up with the feverish pace. According to Don Loughrey, vice-chairman of the X3H2 committee and a standards manager at Hewlett-Packard, "Almost before the ink is dry on one [new standard], we are now writing the standard to replace it. That didn't happen ten years ago. It was all sequential and much slower paced. Today, it's much more parallel, much faster" (Moad, 1990, p. 25). Additionally, "Because technology is advancing so rapidly they [standards committees] often no longer have the luxury of starting off with a handful of proven, tested products from which to form a standard" (Moad, 1990, p. 27). Ballooning committee sizes in combination with this fierce technological advancement, cause many to feel that the standards process needs a complete overhaul. Michael B. Spring, a professor of information sciences at the University of Pittsburgh says, "I have no doubt that anybody who is involved with standards at any level of intensity understands there is a need for changing the process" (Moad, 1990, p. 32).

Unfortunately, even the way the standard was originally written contributed problems to the issue of standardization. One of these inherent problems is that "the ANSI/SQL standard establishes a common target for the many SQL vendors, but it by no means precisely defines a single, all-inclusive language" (Van Name &

Catchings, 1989, p. 175). Others criticize the vagueness in the ANSI standard, which does a good job of specifying the language's syntax (grammar) but a bad job of nailing down its semantics (what the commands actually do)" (Glass, 1991, p. 514). Additional differences "crop up in APIs (application programming interfaces) - interfaces between SQL and application programs written in languages such as C or Cobol" (Glass, 1991, p. S14).

According to E.F. Codd, the father of the relational model, several of the most significant flaws in SQL lie in its original design. Codd has identified three flaws that he has termed fatal. His first criticism is that SQL permits duplicate rows in relations. He deems this a serious weakness since it violates the original relational model and also permits uncontrolled redundancy. Secondly, Codd criticizes SQL for supporting an inadequately defined kind of nesting of a query within a query. His objection here is that by allowing one query to contain other subqueries the user becomes responsible for ensuring adequate performance. Consequently, "the difference in performance in nested and non-nested versions of the same query puts an unnecessary performance-oriented burden on users, which will not disappear until nesting is prohibited" (Codd, 1988a, p. 48). Codd's third reproof of SQL is that it does not adequately support three-valued logic, which is the support for null values in addition to true and false. That is, in any Boolean expression true and false are valid results. However, Codd argues that a null value, resulting from a query that retrieves a record in which one or more of the columns is blank, is not adequately supported. He believes that this lack of support places the undue burden of devising three-valued logic on the user rather than on the DBMS, where he asserts that it belongs. Because of this, he maintains that "users are liable to make numerous mistakes if they are forced to support three-valued logic mentally" (Codd, 1988b, p. 72).

One of Codd's colleagues, C.J. Date, also finds fundamental flaws in the design of SQL. He states that "it cannot be denied that SQL in its present form leaves rather a lot to be desired--even that, in some important respects, it fails to realize the full potential of the relational model" (Date, 1989, p. 5). Date contends that, "although there are well-established principles for the design of formal languages, there is little evidence that SQL was ever designed in accordance with any such principles" (Date, 1989, p. 5). He also feels that several specific functions, such as a DROP TABLE function, were omitted from SQL's original design.

In its original design, problems such as lack of support for necessary functions, idiosyncrasies in its semantics, and flaws in its programming interfaces have haunted SQL. During its evolution, the emergence of a plethora of SQL dialects has contributed to its shortcomings. These issues, in conjunction with rapidly changing technology and the need for support on multiple software and hardware platforms, have contributed to SQL's tempestuous history. Although the reproofs are varied, the absence of a true standard appears to be a common thread in the majority of these difficulties. Pascal encapsulates this theme by saying, "What is badly needed is an improved, fully relational SQL standard that leads, not follows the market" (Pascal, 1989b, p. 256).

2.7 Possible Solutions to SQL Problems

In response to these many problems involving the interoperability of SQL, "A group of companies, including INGRES, Sun Microsystems, Digital Equipment, and Tandem Computers, began meeting informally to discuss how to achieve interoperability and portability of SQL-based RDBMSes" (Crutchfield, 1990, p. 195). This industry coalition felt that although the work of ANSI and ISO was both necessary and meaningful, it did not accomplish the ultimate goal of fully supported SQL compatibility. For this reason, the SQL Access Group was formed in 1989. "The Group's mission is to develop a technical specification that will allow one vendor's SQL application to access data in other vendors' SQL servers, thus enabling RDBMSes and application tools from different vendors to work together" (Crutchfield, 1990, p. 195). Currently a partial solution to the problem of interoperability can be achieved by buying or building "a front-end program that hides the differences between various manufacturers' SQL engines" (Glass, 1991, p. S14). These gateways must be written by both the data base vendor and the application programmers so that one product can communicate with another. This solution's shortcoming, however, is that each client must create a gateway for every SQL server, and each server must create a gateway for every client. Consequently, the number of necessary connections equals the number of clients times the number of servers (see Figure 2) (Crutchfield, 1990, p. 196).

However, if the SQL Access Group's recommendations are adopted, each vendor would be required to provide only one gateway, which would allow access to a true industry standard. As also shown in Figure 2, the number of connections

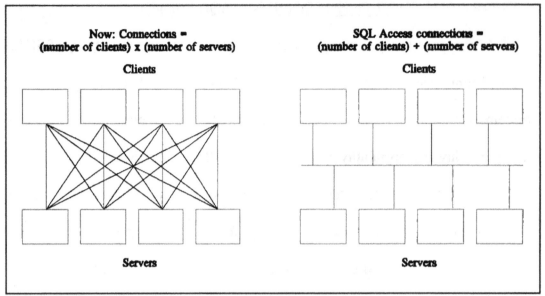

Figure 2 The Solutions

necessary under this solution would equal the number of clients plus the number of servers. This proposed solution directly addresses the problems of multiple software and hardware platforms, SQL dialects, and communication protocols.

The additional problems associated with rapidly changing technology and the outdated standardization processes currently used by ANSI are being dealt with successfully by at least one industry organization. "The IEEE POSIX (The Institute of Electrical and Electronics Engineers Inc. Portable Operating System Interface for UNIX) Working Group, in just five years, built an impressive record for responding to user and vendor requirements rapidly and working with standards consortia" (Moad, 1990, p. 27). According to IEEE officials, one fundamental reason for its successful development of a standard has been its ability to solicit strong user involvement. "According to Paul Borrill, the IEEE Computer Society's Vice President for Standards, many users feel more effective on the POSIX technical committee because, under IEEE rules, all voting is done on an individual rather than an institutional basis. 'The users get the same vote as the manufacturers in the meetings,' says Borrill" (Moad, 1990, p. 27). According to the University of Pittsburgh's Michael B. Spring, a professor in the information sciences department, the standardization process can be successful even in a rapidly changing environment if the standards are developed "closest to the end user" (Moad, 1990, p. 27).

Although the solutions for the problems in the implementation of SQL are relatively focused, the range of suggested solutions for SQL's original design flaws varies widely. According to Codd, the problem of duplicate rows, or duplicate records, should be treated in three phases. First, users should be warned that support for duplicate rows will be phased out over a specified period of time. Secondly, a software switch should be installed in new software releases that would allow the DBMS to operate in two different modes: one mode that permits duplicate rows and a second mode that rejects them. Thirdly, Codd believes that after the specified period of time, duplicate row support should be dropped altogether. Another problem that Codd identified, that of inadequately defined nested queries within queries, should be completely revamped, even to the point of creating an entirely new relational language with ease of user properties being its paramount objective. Codd also feels that support for four-valued logic should be implemented so that the IS NULL clause could be phased out (Codd, 1988b, p. 74). Beech's approach to resolving these design flaws is a much broader one. He states, "If SQL develops as suggested into a more general language that includes the relational model within it, existing users of SQL can plan for evolutionary growth rather than face the specter of future incompatible migration" (Beech, 1989b, p. 48). His proposed expansion of SQL includes such progressive ideas as incorporating an object data model, which he believes would capitalize on the advantages of OOPS (Object Oriented Programming Systems). Other authors feel that the solution is much more concise. According to Trimble, "The solution is obvious: Standardize. Develop one version of SQL supported by all vendors, which can be used on all systems. A standard version of the language would make life much simpler for its users (the effect on SQL *vendors* is more problematic, but at least in theory, it's the users who have the final say)" (Trimble & Chappell, 1989, p. 8). Although none of SQL's problems appears to be irreconcilable since many proposed solutions exist, reaching a consensus on these proposals will be an arduous process. ANSI is continually working on these issues, and, as of this writing, has proposed standards for SQL2 that are currently awaiting approval by organizations such as the ISO. SQL3, an extension that may include object data typing, is already being developed and will most probably be ready for review and acceptance as early as 1993. Clearly, the process by which SQL evolves is occurring at an accelerated pace in order to incorporate the most modern methods of managing relational data bases.

2.8 Summary

In this chapter, the history and background of relational data bases have been addressed. Additionally, the benefits and disadvantages of the query language SQL have been enumerated along with some proposed solutions to the criticisms. The following chapter, Chapter 3, will cover the fundamentals of the SQL language which will be used for the construction industry extensions described in Chapter 4.

CHAPTER 3
FUNDAMENTALS OF SQL

While the previous chapter covered the history and background of SQL this chapter's purpose is to acquaint the reader with the essential principles and syntactic structure of SQL. This understanding is a prerequisite for extending SQL to encompass functions and capabilities necessary to address the informational needs of the construction industry. This extension is both desirable and necessary since currently no extensions to SQL exist that address the industry-specific vocabulary of the construction industry. By addressing this unique vocabulary productivity gains can be achieved through more efficient searches of relational data bases. In this chapter, an overview of the basic principles of SQL is provided first, followed by a synopsis of the three primary functions of the language. Third, the seven relational operators are examined, and finally, the concepts of keys and keywords are addressed.

3.1 Basic Principles of SQL

Prior to comprehending CI-SQL, a fundamental understanding of the relational model and its access language, SQL, is essential. Codd's relational model, as outlined in Chapter 2, sets forth both the precepts and the structure of relational data bases. According to Wipper, "A relational data base is characterized by its simplicity of data management, independence of logical user views from the physical data storage structure, and the availability of simple but powerful relational operators" (Wipper, 1989, p. 27). These characteristics translate into a collection of tables that are composed of rows and columns. Rows, also called tuples, contain the data associated with each of the tables' columns. "Each column in a table is assigned a unique name and contains a particular type of data" (Trimble & Chappell, 1989, p. 3), such as an employee number for each employee in a personnel file. Acting conceptually as a storage medium, the intersections of rows and columns, sometimes called fields, provide the vehicle necessary for locating and accessing relational data. The number of rows in a given table is referred to as the cardinality of that table. The number of columns is called the degree (Date, 1989, p. 25). These rows and columns form two types of tables. The first type, a base table, may be thought of as a table that actually exists; whereas a viewed table, or view, is a virtual table that is extracted from a single base table or a combination of base tables. Another relational data base component, the catalog, "is a system data base containing information about base tables, views, access rights, user-ids, etc. that can be queried through the use of SQL SELECT statements" (Hursch & Hursch, 1988, p. 10).

3.2 Functions of SQL

The relational sublanguage, SQL, provides support for three general functions. First, SQL acts as a Data Definition Language (DDL), which is used for defining the structure of the data. Secondly, it serves as a Data Manipulation Language (DML), which is used for modifying data within the data base. Finally, SQL is a Data Control Language (DCL), which controls user access by specifying security constraints (Hursch & Hursch, 1988, p. 9). By providing these three general functions, SQL allows sophisticated data management processes to be performed on data bases that are based upon highly orthogonal yet simple principles.

3.3 SQL Relational Operators

The tools used for performing these data management processes are termed relational operators. The operators that are supported by the relational model are UNION, INTERSECTION, DIFFERENCE, PRODUCT, PROJECTION, JOIN, and SELECT. Of these operators, only PRODUCT, PROJECTION, JOIN, and SELECT may be performed on tables with differing structures.

3.3.1 UNION Operator

As its name implies, the UNION operator allows the user to combine two tables to create a third resulting table. To perform this function, both tables must have the same number of columns with identical headings and data types for each column. Therefore, the resulting table contains as many rows of information as the sum of the rows of the two initial tables less any duplicate rows. An example of a UNION operation is illustrated in Figure 3.

3.3.2 INTERSECTION Operator

Like the UNION operator, the INTERSECTION operator requires that both tables used in this function be identical in structure but not in content. The table resulting from the INTERSECTION command contains data that was common to both initial tables. Therefore, if the initial tables had no common data, the resulting table would be empty. Given in Figure 4 is an example of an INTERSECTION function.

Store A

Description	Item #	Item Cost	Item Price
3/4" CDX Plywd	0896	$6.45	$8.25
Nail Apron	0766	$13.22	$15.99
Claw Hammer	2265	$8.96	$9.99

UNION

Store B

Description	Item #	Item Cost	Item Price
1/2" Drywall	3244	$7.55	$8.95
Nail Apron	0766	$13.22	$15.99
Roofing Hammer	3341	$9.36	$11.99

Produces:

Stores A and B

Description	Item #	Item Cost	Item Price
3/4" CDX Plywd	0896	$6.45	$8.25
Nail Apron	0766	$13.22	$15.99
Claw Hammer	2265	$8.96	$9.99
1/2" Drywall	3244	$7.55	$8.95
Roofing Hammer	3341	$9.36	$11.99

Figure 3 The UNION Operator

Store A

Description	Item #	Item Cost	Item Price
3/4" CDX Plywd	0896	$6.45	$8.25
Nail Apron	0766	$13.22	$15.99
Claw Hammer	2265	$8.96	$9.99

INTERSECTION

Store B

Description	Item #	Item Cost	Item Price
1/2" Drywall	3244	$7.55	$8.95
Nail Apron	0766	$13.22	$15.99
Roofing Hammer	3341	$9.36	$11.99

Produces:

Stores A and B

Description	Item #	Item Cost	Item Price
Nail Apron	0766	$13.22	$15.99

Figure 4   The INTERSECTION Operator

3.3.3 DIFFERENCE Operator

Unlike UNION and INTERSECTION, the results of a DIFFERENCE operation are directly affected by the order in which the original tables are accessed. For example, DIFFERENCE can be used to locate all rows that exist in table one but not in table two. This operation, however, would not produce the same results as locating all rows that occur in table two but not table one. The example shown in Figure 5 demonstrates the use of the DIFFERENCE operator.

Store A

Description	Item #	Item Cost	Item Price
3/4" CDX Plywd	0896	$6.45	$8.25
Nail Apron	0766	$13.22	$15.99
Claw Hammer	2265	$8.96	$9.99

DIFFERENCE

Store B

Description	Item #	Item Cost	Item Price
1/2" Drywall	3244	$7.55	$8.95
Nail Apron	0766	$13.22	$15.99
Roofing Hammer	3341	$9.36	$11.99

Produces:

Only Store A

Description	Item #	Item Cost	Item Price
3/4" CDX Plywd	0896	$6.45	$8.25
Claw Hammer	2265	$8.96	$9.99

and

Only Store B

Description	Item #	Item Cost	Item Price
1/2" Drywall	3244	$7.55	$8.95
Roofing Hammer	3341	$9.36	$11.99

Figure 5 The DIFFERENCE Operator

3.3.4 PRODUCT Operator

PRODUCT is the first of four relational operators that can be performed on tables with differing structures. This function produces a table that contains all possible combinations of the rows in the two original tables. For example, if the three primary models of Honda automobiles were contained in one table, and all four exterior color choices were listed in a second table, the table resulting from a PRODUCT operation would contain twelve rows listing all possible combinations. This example is given in Figure 6.

3.3.5 PROJECTION Operator

Unlike the previously discussed operators, a PROJECTION can be performed on a single table. The PROJECTION operation permits the selection of specified columns from an existing table. Therefore, PROJECTION produces a table with fewer columns than its source table. For example, employee number and race could be listed in a PROJECTION table that was derived from a detailed personnel file. This illustration is shown in Figure 7.

3.3.6 JOIN Operator

Like the PRODUCT operator, JOIN also creates a new table that contains data from the two original tables. However, a JOIN condition must first be satisfied in order to perform this operation. The most common JOIN condition is called an equi-join. In this case, values from specified columns must be equal in order to satisfy the JOIN condition. Consequently, the table derived from an equi-join operation contains concatenated rows that had some common value in the source

Models

Model	Model #	Cost	Price
Prelude	1244	$17,233	$22,821
Accord	2776	$14,356	$18,189
Civic	3220	$9,976	$11,821

PRODUCT

Color	Color #
Blue	B165
Green	J323
White	W459
Gray	G921

Produces:

Model	Model #	Cost	Price	Color	Color #
Prelude	1244	$17,233	$22,821	Blue	B165
Prelude	1244	$17,233	$22,821	Green	GN323
Prelude	1244	$17,233	$22,821	White	W459
Prelude	1244	$17,233	$22,821	Gray	G921
Accord	2776	$14,356	$18,189	Blue	B165
Accord	2776	$14,356	$18,189	Green	GN323
Accord	2776	$14,356	$18,189	White	W459
Accord	2776	$14,356	$18,189	Gray	G921
Civic	3220	$9,976	$11,821	Blue	B165
Civic	3220	$9,976	$11,821	Green	GN323
Civic	3220	$9,976	$11,821	White	W459
Civic	3220	$9,976	$11,821	Gray	G921

Figure 6 The PRODUCT Operator

tables. For instance, if table one detailed the model, weight, and color of an automobile inventory, and table two listed colors, and their associated paint numbers, the process of equi-join on color would appear as shown in Figure 8.

Last	First	Emp. ID #	Sex	Race
Smith	David	1122	M	B
Richards	Michelle	3442	F	W
Gonzales	Juan	8127	M	H
Brett	Mary	6310	F	W
Harkins	Allison	5528	F	B

Produces:

Emp. ID #	Race
1122	B
3442	W
8127	H
6310	W
5528	B

Figure 7 The PROJECTION Operator

Model	Weight	Color
Corolla	2600	Blue
Cressida	3215	White
Supra	3312	Gray
Corona	2788	Black
Camry	3190	Red

Join

Color	Paint #
Blue	132
White	212
Gray	234
Black	621
Red	517

Produces:

Model	Weight	Color	Paint #
Corolla	2600	Blue	132
Cressida	3215	White	212
Supra	3312	Gray	234
Corona	2788	Black	621
Camry	3190	Red	517

Figure 8 The JOIN Operator

3.3.7 SELECT Operator

The final and most frequently used relational operator is SELECT. Since the primary purpose of any query language is the retrieval of data from the data base, the SELECT statement is clearly at the core of SQL. Instead of selecting specific columns of data as the PROJECTION operator does, SELECT purposes to choose rows of data. The general form of SELECT is

SELECT <column name(s)>

FROM <table>

WHERE <constraint(s)>

where <column name(s)> represents the specific columns that are to be extracted from the table specified in the FROM clause. WHERE is an optional clause that allows the user to institute further constraints on the query. A Boolean expression is used in the WHERE clause as a tool for evaluating data to determine whether it fits the given set of conditions. This condition, or Boolean expression, is called the predicate. Examples of predicates are EXISTS, (NOT EXISTS), >, <=, and BETWEEN...AND.... The following is an example of the SELECT operator:

SELECT salesman, region, gross_sales

FROM Sales

WHERE gross_sales > 100,000

When this SELECT operation is performed on the Sales Table the results are as shown in Figure 9.

Sales Table

Salesman	Region	Supervisor	Age	Gross Sales
Smith	NE	D. Jones	36	75,000
Arnold	SE	L. Brown	44	123,450
Drake	SW	B. Benson	51	112,500
Samuels	NW	R. Rogers	29	88,300

Salesman	Region	Gross Sales
Arnold	SE	123,450
Drake	SW	112,500

Figure 9 The SELECT Operator

Through the use of these seven relational operators, powerful queries can be formulated in both nested and non-nested forms to extract necessary data from relational data bases.

3.4 SQL Keys and Keywords

Two additional instruments provide for searching and query construction in the SQL environment: keys and key words. Since the rows in a relational data base are unordered, and efficient searches are of supreme importance, a device must exist for rapidly locating desired data. This device, called a key, performs this function. An individual column or columns may be designated as the key(s) for a particular table which requires that each value in the key column be unique. This ensures that searching the data base takes place in an expedient, rather than random fashion.

Finally, like most programming languages, SQL retains a list of several words that may not be used in tables or column names. Figure 10 lists SQL's key words (Trimble & Chappell, 1989, p. 12).

ALL	AND	ANY	AS
ASC	AUTHORIZATION	AVG	BEGIN
BETWEEN	BY	CHAR	CHARACTER
CHECK	CLOSE	COBOL	COMMIT
CONTINUE	COUNT	CREATE	CURRENT
CURSOR	DEC	DECIMAL	DECLARE
DELETE	DESC	DISTINCT	DOUBLE
END	ESCAPE	EXEC	EXISTS
FETCH	FLOAT	FOR	FORTRAN
FOUND	FROM	GO	GOTO
GRANT	GROUP	HAVING	IN
INDICATOR	INSERT	INT	INTEGER
INTO	IS	LANGUAGE	LIKE
MAX	MIN	MODULE	NOT
NULL	NUMERIC	OF	ON
OPEN	OPTION	OR	ORDER
PASCAL	PLI	PRECISION	PRIVILEGES
PROCEDURE	PUBLIC	REAL	ROLLBACK
SCHEMA	SECTION	SELECT	SET
SMALLINT	SOME	SQL	SQLCODE
SQLERROR	SUM	TABLE	TO
UNION	UNIQUE	UPDATE	USER

Figure 10 SQL Keywords

Clearly, there is not an attempt in this chapter to examine the complete structure and the many nuances of SQL. However, sufficient framework has been established such that an extension of this query language can be undertaken in the subsequent chapter. This extension will preserve all components of the relational model and SQL discussed in this chapter, adding only those modifications necessary to make it specific to the construction industry.

3.5 Summary

In Chapter 3 the fundamental structure of SQL queries has been described. This description is key to providing a basis for the extensions to be undertaken in the following chapter. Several simple examples were also given to clarify the usage of the primary SQL operators. Chapter 4 will detail the extensions that have been designed to be directly applicable to queries that are particularly useful to the construction industry in order to achieve a more efficient and intuitive method of querying construction data bases.

CHAPTER 4
FRAMEWORK FOR SQL EXTENSIONS

With the foundational syntax of SQL having been reviewed in the previous chapter, the power and simplicity of this relational query language should be evident. It is this combination of characteristics that has caused SQL to be adopted as an industry standard and is the primary motivation for using this language as the basis for the construction industry-specific extensions. In creating these extensions the purpose of this research is not to develop a new relational query language, to develop a new software package, or to completely revamp the most widely accepted relational data base query language. Many authors and relational data base experts have thoroughly covered such territory in both theory and practice. The intent of this research is, however, to develop a new conceptual model of construction industry-specific extensions upon which subsequent research and applications can be generated. Aimed at extending construction research and improving the handling of construction information, this research focuses on industry-specific extensions that have not yet been addressed. The primary benefit of this research for the construction industry will be improved productivity in the area of information retrieval. The productivity gains will be realized through the creation of simple, more effective methods of querying relational data bases. Presently, many design and construction professionals may not be using SQL due to the resemblance it bears to a programming language. By adding construction-specific vocabulary this apparent aversion could be overcome and the construction industry could begin to tap into the power and efficiency of the standard in relational query languages. It is important to note, however, that this research only begins the process of simplifying relational queries for the construction industry. Many other issues, as addressed in section 1.2, must be resolved in order to complete the work of tailoring SQL for use by construction professionals.

The remainder of this chapter is organized into several major divisions. Section 4.1 examines other extensions to SQL and their results. Section 4.2 defines what CI-SQL is and how it compares/contrasts to the ANSI version of SQL. In section 4.3 the concepts of object data typing are described as they relate to possible applications in the construction industry. Section 4.4 contains an explanation of Beech's main concepts of correlating relational data bases to object data base management systems. Section 4.5 blends object data base management concepts with the application of user-defined functions using a construction-specific case. Finally, sections 4.6 and 4.7 briefly review the SQL3 method of defining functions and the conventions used in extending the syntax of SQL. With these explanations in place, the reader will have the necessary foundation for the extensions that will be detailed in Chapter 5.

4.1 Previous SQL Extensions

Several previous efforts have been directed at extending SQL in various areas, particularly in the representation of spatial data. In 1985 Sikeler proposed that SQL be extended to encompass the treatment of spatial relations and the use of a picture list to manage graphical output. That same year Roussopoulos (Egenhofer, 1989, p.

79) developed PSQL (Pictorial SQL) in which two clauses were added to the SELECT-FROM-WHERE construct. In his work, Egenhofer criticizes this extension for making "the formulation of queries unnecessarily complicated" (Egenhofer, 1989, p. 79). In 1987 Ingram added syntax extensions to SQL to address the needs of geographic information systems. However, in this work, Ingram (Egenhofer, 1989, p. 79) also added a command set outside of ANSI supported SQL. The following year Herring (Egenhofer, 1989, p. 80) pursued an object-oriented approach to extending SQL but sacrificed some SQL principles in the process. In 1989 Egenhofer attempted unsuccessfully to combine spatial concepts with a graphical user interface. By his own admission his work culminated in "a negative demonstration of the extension of an SQL-like language for spatial data handling" (Egenhofer, 1989, p. 161). Although several attempts have been made at extending SQL in application specific areas, no published undertakings exist in handling construction information.

4.2 Nature of CI-SQL

Unlike some of the works cited in the previous section, CI-SQL will preserve all of the functionality and regulations of the ANSI supported version. By doing so, complete compatibility is maintained with existing implementations that use the ANSI standard. Maintaining complete compatibility is essential in order to ensure that this work is a true extension which augments rather than replaces an existing standard. The additions proposed in this work will be in the form of semantic rather than syntactical changes. This constraint means that instead of altering the structure of SQL commands and keywords, construction-specific vocabulary will be used to create new commands that adhere to the existing SQL pattern. Because this extension occurs in an area in which SQL rarely has been applied, the existing field of compatible relational data bases will be meager. For this reason a generic data base structure will be explained using a construction material example for illustration.

The role that CI-SQL plays in providing information retrieval facilities for the construction industry is that of an intermediary. CI-SQL begins the process of bridging the gap between construction data and the construction professional. In order for a user to access a data base, a query language must be provided as the tool for achieving this access. Here, CI-SQL acts as the intermediary between the user and the data, possibly through the use of a user interface. The user interface would provide a more intuitive method of accessing the data without requiring the user to become an expert at formulating SQL queries. This interface would also address the cliche, but relevant, issue of user-friendliness. For users who are unfamiliar with query languages, a user-friendly interface could conceal the actual process of building SQL queries. Because this research does not attempt to address the development of a user interface, further research is certainly warranted in this area. It should also be noted that this research is not purported to be the culmination of a process, but rather the commencement of the effort necessary to supply a complete CI-SQL.

4.3 Object Data Typing

Although the purpose of this dissertation is by no means to address comprehensively the addition of object data typing and user-defined functions to the SQL language, it is vital to this work to develop the conceptual foundation upon which the construction industry's extensions are built. The following object data model concepts are primarily based upon the work of Oracle Corporation's David

Beech, who has been particularly outspoken regarding the specific benefits to be derived from such an addition. In their paper, "Object data bases as generalizations of relational data bases," Beech and Ozbutun propose that the object data model should subsume rather than replace or be appended to the relational model. By approaching object data modeling in this fashion, they believe that the relational concepts and benefits of the existing SQL standard can be preserved and improved rather than creating an entirely new language. Thus, "an object data base management system (ODBMS) could then contain within it all the functionality of a relational data base management system (RDBMS)" (Beech & Ozbutun, 1991, p. 221). The use of object data bases and their comparably simple syntax potentially could overcome many of the difficulties associated with the syntactic complexity of standard relational query languages. Through the implementation of the Entity-Relationship (E-R) model a much more intuitive approach to relational data base modeling can be achieved. In the E-R model, the relationships between entities are described, rather than using keys to model connections between columns. For example, this approach "allows the user to describe both entities such as Employees and Departments, and relationships between them such as WorksIn" (Beech, 1989b, p. 45). Thus, the intent of this chapter is to develop the framework within which the construction industry-specific extensions will exist.

4.4 Objects, Identity, and Attributes

This development is reliant upon an understanding of some of Beech's main concepts. Fundamentally, an object data base is a collection of information objects. Each object, or instance, can be directly mapped to a tuple, or row, in the relational model. This correlation provides a smooth transition from the strictly relational model to one which incorporates the characteristics of an object data base. In addition to describing tuples as objects, each object has both identity and attributes. The principle of identity is that although the characteristics, or attributes, of an object may change over time, it is still the same object. For example, although an employee's department and address may change, the object itself is still an employee. The concept of attributes is most easily explained through the use of an example. A person object may have such attributes as name, address, and birthdate that characterize and uniquely identify that object (see Figure 11) (Beech & Ozbutun, 1991, p. 222).

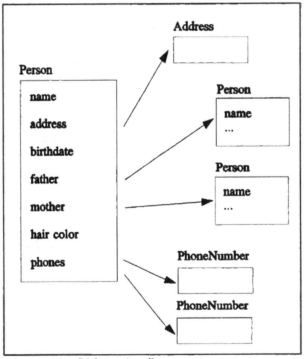

Figure 11 Object Attributes

Beech further elaborates that the concept of classes brings together an object's characteristics and behavior, thus creating a template, or form, from which subsequent objects of the same type, called instances, may be created. This principle of inheritance means that when a new instance is created from an existing class, it inherits the attributes and operations, or functions, of that class. These principles of object oriented data bases are being woven into SQL to develop a richer and more powerful relational data base language.

4.5 User-Defined Functions

In addition to providing embedded construction-specific functions, one of the most desirable extensions to SQL proposed in this research is the capability of creating construction-specific, user-defined data types, objects, and functions. Due to the specialized nature of construction data bases and queries, the ability to construct and reuse functions that are application specific is of enormous benefit to the end user. By providing this facility the queries can be tailored to construction industry data bases as well as the individual query needs of the user. The following is a sample scenario that demonstrates the need and details the creation process of a user-defined function.

During the design phase of a construction project, project specifications are created to detail the materials and methods to be used during construction in order to provide the level of quality desired by the owner and his or her architect. In the process of creating these specifications the designer may enumerate literally thousands of products or materials and the particular characteristics that they should possess. Again, the nature of this process lends itself very well to the use of object data typing since object data types have attributes just as the physical objects they represent do. To this end, furnishing the data base user with object data typing facilities and user-definable functions will allow for the construction of complex industry-specific queries that are not currently provided for in SQL.

In creating a user-defined function the following two distinct steps are involved:

1. Define the object type

2. Create an instance or instances of the object type.

The initial step in creating a user-defined function that maintains the properties of the object oriented data base management system is the object type definition. This step creates the template or class from which other objects having the same properties can be created. In this example several of the critical attributes of wood doors are used to create the object type WoodDoor. It should be noted that in these constructions existing SQL vocabulary is shown in uppercase letters, while additions to the syntax are shown in bold type. Object types begin with a capital letter whereas their instances begin with a lowercase letter. After each attribute, or field, is defined its data type is characterized. For instance, in the following example the attribute Manufacturer is defined as a character string of up to fifteen characters (CHAR(15)).

CREATE **type** WoodDoor

(Manufacturer CHAR(15),

Model# CHAR(10),

Face_material CHAR(20),

Core_material CHAR(20),

Edge_material CHAR(20));

Once the object type has been created the user is able to create actual objects, or instances, of the object type. Here, an instance of WoodDoor is woodDoor and is created as follows:

CREATE woodDoor

instance ('Pella', 'SCO-30', 'oak', 'particle board', 'multi-ply laminated')

This process of creating an instance of WoodDoor, as with any object type, is accomplished much like the insertion of a row into a conventional relational table. However, instead of using the keyword INSERT, CREATE is used since the concept of "creating" an instance, or object, may be much more intuitive to the user. For each of the attributes defined in the creation of the object type, or class, the instance command inserts the subsequent values into the type definition parameters.

The final step in providing a user-defined function is the procedure of creating the function itself. The justification for such a development and addition to the existing body of SQL functions is that the ability to create application specific functions would greatly enhance the power and usability of SQL for industry professionals. Since the purpose of SQL is information retrieval, the more a user can customize the query language to meet his informational needs the more powerful that language becomes. Thus, "the goal is to make the modeling of information as direct and natural as possible, and to overcome the impedance mismatch with programming languages that already have many of these richer facilities" (Beech, 1989b, p. 45). For this reason a suggested procedure for creating user-defined functions is given below. Although the example presented here may be limited in scope it demonstrates the potential application of user-defined functions in directly meeting an industry-specific need for information retrieval. If, as is common practice, an architect intended to specify the doors in a project based upon the materials that composed the face, core, and edge, or stile, of the door, the following function would allow him to search a construction data base and retrieve all products that met his criteria.

CREATE function *select_door* (face, core, edge) as

SELECT manufacturer, model#

FROM Division_8_Doors&Windows

WHERE face_material = face

AND core_material = core

AND edge_material = edge

By specifying the arguments face, core and edge, this function would return the manufacturer and model number of all products in the Division_8_Doors&Windows data base that met the given criteria.

By developing a robust collection of such user-defined, industry-specific functions, the procedure of retrieving data in a vertical market data base could be thoroughly customized. This customization could thus enhance and simplify an industry-specific query language to the point that knowledge of the industry's vernacular could largely replace a detailed knowledge of SQL syntax. The net result of this simplification would be that the information contained in the data base would be brought much closer to the end user.

4.6 SQL3 Function Definition

In its current state of development, SQL3 function definitions are accomplished as follows:

```
<SQL function> ::=

    [<function type>] FUNCTION <SQL function name>

        <parameter declaration list>

    RETURNS <SQL function result>

    <SQL statement>;

    END FUNCTION
```

where

```
<function type> ::= CONSTRUCTOR | ACTOR | DESTRUCTOR

<parameter declaration list> ::= <parameter declaration>

                                | (<parameter declaration> [,...])

<parameter declaration> ::= <parameter name> <data type>

                          | SQLCODE

                          | SQLSTATE
```

The following restrictions are placed upon these functions:

1) all SQL functions with the same name must have the same corresponding parameter modes

2) all SQL functions must contain a RETURN statement

3) <function type> must be used in Abstract Data Type (ADT) definition and nowhere else

4) constructor functions must have appropriate <new statement>

5) destructor functions must have appropriate <destroy statement>

4.7 Syntax Conventions

Additionally, the following syntax conventions apply to all extensions contained in the following chapter:

1) function names are italicized and not capitalized

2) object types or classes, as well as data base names, are capitalized

3) data base fields or object instances are not capitalized

4.8 Summary

This chapter has set forth a format for the development of construction-specific extensions to SQL. Previous attempts at extending SQL have been described and their successes and failures have been noted. A framework for the nature of CI-SQL has also been characterized, including the features of object data typing applicable to CI-SQL. The following chapter will detail the actual extensions that comprise CI-SQL and give query examples to illustrate their uses.

CHAPTER 5
CONSTRUCTION-SPECIFIC SQL EXTENSIONS

The preceding chapter has defined the parameters for the development of construction-specific extensions to SQL. Within this framework, this chapter will detail the extensions included in CI-SQL. The first and largest domain in which SQL extensions are created is in the area of construction materials. This application is developed in section 5.1 with the specific extensions. Within this section the hypothetical general data base structure for construction materials is described. Also, assumptions regarding the extensions are contained in section 5.1. The subsequent section, 5.2, develops the second major domain of construction-specific SQL extensions. This section also includes a description of the general data base structure, and the assumptions necessary for creating the extensions, as well as the applicable basic scheduling concepts. The final section, 5.3, summarizes the extensions that were developed for CI-SQL.

5.1 Construction Materials Domain

The first major domain of construction-specific SQL extensions has been developed to address the unique query needs of construction material and product selection. Due to the complex nature of the data base itself, the need for vernacular query capabilities is significant. Merely organizing the data does not sufficiently meet the informational needs of the construction professional. The ability to query the data base using vocabulary currently familiar to the typical user is necessary in order to maximize the use of this powerful relational tool. Using terminology very common to actual project specifications (see Appendix A), these extensions were developed to provide construction-specific functions for information retrieval. This set of extensions will be developed in the following format: first, each function will be described along with the need or motivation for its development; second, the function's syntax will be detailed; third, a sample query will be given followed by the formal representation of the query; finally, the result of the query will be provided in standard tabular form.

5.1.1 General Materials Data Base Structure

The general concepts of relational data base design clearly apply to the creation of a complex construction materials data base. First, the idea that all relational data can, and must, be represented in the form of tables at the logical level simplifies the process of structuring the data while representing it in a familiar form. Second, "the decoupling of logical and physical levels means that logical and physical design problems can be separately addressed" (Date, 1988b, p. 18). The logical level of design addresses how the data is structured and retrieved while the physical design addresses how the data is actually stored on disk. Third, normalization, or the process of simplifying data structures into simple relations, ensures that the structure of the data is in its simplest form. Finally, the ability to dynamically define data coupled with the independent nature of relational data means that the design process can be ongoing and has a forgiving nature. However, due to the complexity of a full-featured construction materials data base, it would be unreasonable to detail the format of a data base that would contain all applicable divisions of the construction materials domain as systematized by the Construction Specifications Institute (CSI). By conforming the data base to the sixteen divisions enumerated in the CSI MasterSpec format (see Appendix B), compatibility with current construction conventions and familiarity to construction professionals can be preserved while maintaining the simplicity of the relational model.

Based on this premise a natural division of data bases begins to emerge. For illustrative purposes, the general data base structure of an industry standard product data base, Sweet's SweetSearch Building Product Search System on CD-ROM (see Appendix C), will be used as the basis for sample relational queries. It should be noted that although Sweet's data base does not currently support SQL queries it is highly probable that a "live" or on-line version of this product or a similar one would, by necessity, support the SQL standard. Using Division 8, Doors and Windows as an example, the following is a description of the general pattern that would characterize such a data base. In the definition of any construction materials data base schema the typical characteristics of the general class of materials would have to be clearly defined. In this example, doors and windows, the two materials belonging to this class would have to be separated into two distinct divisions: 1) doors and 2) windows. Within each division the attributes indigenous to that material would become fields in the data base. For example, doors would be either wood or metal, flush or paneled, and hollow or solid core. This procedure would begin to categorize the doors into specific groupings that would differentiate one door from another. The next level of detail might characterize the thickness, width, and height of a specific door and designate whether it had lites or louvers. The data base specification could also be designed to include performance qualities such as fire resistance and sound transmission properties. These attribute templates must be generated for each class of materials in order to map properly a data base design to the actual characteristics of the construction material. In the case of Sweet's Building Product Search System, these templates have been created for all sixteen CSI divisions and implemented using an internal search engine.

5.1.2 Extension Assumptions

At this point it becomes necessary to outline several assumptions that must be in place in order to define properly the scope and format of this work. First, it is assumed for the purposes of this research that a data base structure of comparable size and complexity to Sweet's has already been created and does support Structured Query Language searches. Because SQL is the industry standard and an increasing number of data base developers are designing data bases that support this query language, this assumption is exceedingly viable. Second, it also is assumed that any data base of this magnitude would be arranged according to the numbering convention of the Construction Specifications Institute (CSI) since this system has become the de facto standard for dividing construction products, services, and specifications into manageable sections. Third, the general format of this chapter will be to introduce each new extension, describe its application, detail its syntax, and finally, provide an appropriate sample query. It should be noted that in each of the sample queries given in this chapter the purpose of the example is to demonstrate the use the new extension rather than to combine it with other standard SQL modifiers.

Therefore, a typical query used by a construction professional would entail the use of some, if not many, more modifiers in order to retrieve an acceptable body of information. For example, if the user wanted to retrieve a selection of doors, qualifiers such as size, swing, material, height, fire rating and style could all be specified in order to limit the scope of the search.

5.1.3 *complies_with_standard*

The first SQL extension created for construction industry-specific queries is the *complies_with_standard* function which would retrieve all standards to which a particular product conforms. The practical application of this function is twofold. During the design phase, the architect/engineer would be able to use this function to determine which products in a manufacturer's data base meet a particular design standard that he or she has specified. Additionally, during the bidding phase of the project, the contractor could use the same query function on a different data base containing pricing and availability information to determine the cost and availability of a particular product that has been specified by the design team. By providing the ability to return both the standards to which a particular material complies as well as the materials that meet a particular standard, the search capabilities for this scenario would be thoroughly covered. The following syntax extension shows how the first of two extensions are defined by using the particular material in question as the parameter or argument for the function and returning the standard or standards to which it conforms.

Syntax:

complies_with_standard ::=

ACTOR FUNCTION *complies_with_standard* (material REF (Materials))

RETURNS standard;

    RETURN SELECT manufacturer, product, conformance

        FROM Materials

        WHERE product = material

    END FUNCTION

Sample Query:

    Given a data base Division_9_Finishes with an instance acousticalCeilingTile,
list the standard with which Armstrong's ceiling tile, model ACT-22M,
complies.

Query Form:

    SELECT *

    FROM Division_9_Finishes

    WHERE *complies_with_standard* (ACT-22M)

Query Result:

Manufacturer	Product	Conformance
Armstrong	ACT-22M	ASTM E 1264

5.1.4 *material_complies_with*

The second SQL extension, *material_complies_with* is actually a variation of
the *complies_with_standard* function. In this instance the function uses the specified

standard as the argument and returns a list of materials meeting that standard. In the construction industry the application of this function would be in the retrieval of all appropriate materials conforming to a standard specified in the project specifications. For example, if a contractor bidding on a job desired to see a list of all fan motors that conform to a particular UL standard, the following function would provide the necessary capabilities for retrieving the acceptable options. The contractor could then choose from those options while considering such issues as cost and projected delivery time or add such restrictions as predicates in the WHERE clause of the query.

Syntax:

material_complies_with ::=

    ACTOR FUNCTION *material_complies_with* (standard REF (Standards))

    RETURNS material;

    RETURN SELECT conformance, manufacturer, product

        FROM Materials

        WHERE conformance = standard

    END FUNCTION

Sample Query:

    Given a data base Division_9_Finishes with an instance acousticalCeilingTile, list all ceiling tiles that comply with ASTM standard E 1264.

Query Form:

    SELECT *

FROM Division_9_Finishes

WHERE *material_complies_with* (ASTM E 1264)

Query Result:

Conformance	Manufacturer	Product
ASTM E 1264	Armstrong	ACT-22M
ASTM E 1264	Armstrong	ACT-28R
ASTM E 1264	Mannington	MCT0800

In both of the previous models **standard** refers to an instance of the object type **Standard**, which is the class of construction standards. Likewise, **material** is an instance of the object type **Material** which is the class of construction materials. Obviously, depending on the particular subclass of materials or standards being referenced in the query, more specificity would be used in order to access the appropriate data base. For example, if an architect was creating project specifications for Division 8, Doors and Windows, the **material** object might be replaced with a specific instance **woodDoor** of the object type **Doors**. Therefore the models must be expressly tailored to meet the informational needs of the user.

5.1.5 *tested_per_test*

The third construction-specific SQL extension, *tested_per_test*, provides the capability of determining whether a specified product has been subjected to a given test. For example, when specifying fire resistant wire glass, the architect/engineer might require that all wire glass products be tested against UL 9 in order to ensure proper performance in the case of fire. Similarly, the project owner might have a desire to incorporate a particular manufacturer's product with which he has had a high degree of success on previous projects. This function would allow the project owner to determine whether his chosen products met the requirements of the product testing specified by the designer.

Syntax:

tested_per_test ::=

ACTOR FUNCTION *tested_per_test* (manufacturer, material REF (Materials))
RETURNS testing_test;

    RETURN SELECT manufacturer, product, test

        FROM Materials

        WHERE product = material

    END FUNCTION

Sample Query:

    Given a data base Division_8_Doors&Windows with an instance fireResistantWireGlass, list the test, if any, against which ASG Industries' wire glass has been tested.

Query Form:

    SELECT *

    FROM Division_8_Doors&Windows

    WHERE *tested_per_test* (ASG Industries, wire glass)

Query Result:

Manufacturer	Product	Test
ASG Industries	Wire glass	UL 9

5.1.6 material_tested_per

The fourth extension, *material_tested_per*, is a variation of the *tested_per_test* syntax. However, this implementation returns the material or materials that have passed a particular test rather than returning the test against which the material has been tested. The application here is clear in that during the bidding phase of a construction project, a contractor could search a construction data base, retrieving all materials of a given type that have passed the tests specified by the designer. This process would allow the contractor to maximize his profit on the material costs of a job by incorporating materials of equal quality but lower cost than those specified by the architect/engineer.

Syntax:

material_tested_per ::=

ACTOR FUNCTION *material_tested_per* (test)

RETURNS material;

RETURN SELECT test, manufacturer, product

FROM Materials

WHERE test = test

END FUNCTION

Sample Query:

Given a data base Division_8_Doors&Windows with an instance fireResistantWireGlass, list all wire glass products and their manufacturers that have been tested against UL 9.

Query Form:

SELECT *

FROM Division_8_Doors&Windows

WHERE *material_tested_per* (UL 9)

Query Result:

Test	Manufacturer	Product
UL 9	ASG Industries	Wire glass
UL 9	Hordis Brothers	Wire glass

5.1.7 *meets_or_exceeds*

Another material constraint common to project specifications is that a certain attribute of a product must meet or exceed a given value. To address this need, the CI-SQL function *meets_or_exceeds* has been developed. When passed the parameters of product type, attribute, and value, this function returns all products whose specified attribute is greater than or equal to the specified value. As an example, the project architect commonly specifies that a building's heating and air conditioning system must have an EER (energy efficiency ratio) that meets or exceeds a given value.

Syntax:

meets_or_exceeds ::=

ACTOR FUNCTION *meets_or_exceeds* (attribute, value)

RETURNS material;

> RETURN SELECT manufacturer, product, attribute, value
>
> > FROM Materials
> >
> > WHERE attribute $\geq$ value
>
> END FUNCTION

Sample Query:

> Given a data base Division_15_Mechanical with an instance fanMotor, list all
>
> fan motors whose efficiencies meet or exceed 81%.

Query Form:

> SELECT *
>
> FROM Division_15_Mechanical
>
> WHERE *meets_or_exceeds* (efficiency, .81)

Query Result:

Manufacturer	Product	Attribute	Value
Marathon	FM2710	efficiency	.81
US Motors	215EFM	efficiency	.84
GE	EF2117G	efficiency	.84
Westinghouse	WFM-19C2	efficiency	.86

5.1.8 Sample Application

In the previous sections of this chapter, the individual extensions of CI-SQL have been detailed. The purpose of this section is to demonstrate the use of several of these extensions in a combined form. This demonstration will be designed to mimic an actual query that might be required in industry practice. It should be noted that in a total solution a user interface would hide much of the query construction from the user. Again, the data base that would be used for this query is only hypothetical and an actual industry data base might differ significantly depending on the input obtained from product manufacturers and specifiers.

Sample Scenario: The chief estimator for XYZ Construction Company is bidding on an expansion to Liberty Elementary School in Hawthorne, Florida. He has determined from the project drawings that sixteen wood doors will have to be supplied in one wing of the school. These doors must have the following characteristics:

1) Solid Core
2) 1-3/4" Thick
3) 3'0" Wide
4) AWI Grade III
5) Cost less than $250.00 each
6) Primer finish
7) Comply with ASTM E 221
8) Tested per ASTM E 81-S
9) Fire rating that meets or exceeds 1-1/2 hours
10) Acceptable manufacturers are:
    a. Allied Wood Products
    b. TreeCo Corporation
    c. Wood Builders Products Corp.
    d. Florida Door

Based on this information the estimator constructs a query to search the WoodDoors data base for all doors matching the above specifications. The query is structured as shown below.

```
SELECT manufacturer, model, cost

FROM WoodDoor

WHERE   core = 'Solid' AND

   thickness = '1-3/4'' AND

   width = '3'-0'' AND

   awi_grade = 'III' AND

   cost < 250 AND

   finish = 'primer' AND

   complies_with_standard (ASTM E 221) AND

   material_tested_per (ASTM E 81-S) AND

   meets_or_exceeds (fire_rating, 1.5) AND

   manufacturer = 'Allied Wood Products' OR

      'TreeCo Corporation' OR

      'Wood Builders Products' OR

      'Florida Door' AND

   quantity_on_hand ≥ 16

ORDER BY manufacturer, model;
```

The result of this query might be as follows:

Manufacturer	Model	Cost
Allied Wood Products	JL 211-2	228.50
Allied Wood Products	JL 212-5	244.65
Allied Wood Products	JL 297-5	249.85
TreeCo Corporation	TCWD 1156	219.38
Wood Builders Products	W-8972Z	249.99
Wood Builders Products	W-8978Z	235.75

The primary benefit to such query capabilities would be that if a "live" data base were maintained by local or even national suppliers, the architects and contractors would have computerized access to detailed product information. Other beneficial options could be added to the system such as the ability to provide cut sheets, installation information, and pricing structures that depend upon passwords. Clearly, the level of sophistication inherent in such a system is almost limitless. The cost of such sophistication could be supported by both the manufacturers, who have an obvious financial interest, and the construction professionals, who need timely access to large amounts of data.

5.2 Construction Scheduling Domain

The second major domain of construction-specific SQL extensions has been developed to address query needs in area of construction project scheduling. Like material/product selection, construction scheduling lends itself well to a relational data base approach in that a project schedule is composed of activities that have very specific elements of information, or attributes, associated with them. In its simplest form an activity must have a name, a start date, a finish date, and a duration. Using these properties it becomes possible to determine a project's expected completion date. Again, the purpose of this research is not to provide a tutorial on the many facets of construction scheduling using the Critical Path Method (CPM) or the Project Evaluation and Review Technique (PERT), but rather to develop construction-specific extensions to the relational data base query language SQL. With this purpose clarified the following section will develop these extensions in the following format: first, the generic structure of an appropriate data base will be described; second, a review of the basic scheduling concepts necessary for the extensions will be described; third, the assumptions necessary for creating the extensions will be explained; fourth, for each CI-SQL extension a description of the function will be provided as well as the need or motivation for its development; fifth, the exact syntax will be detailed; next, a sample query will be created followed by the formal representation of the query; finally, the result of the query will be provided.

5.2.1 Basic Scheduling Concepts

Regardless of which planning method is used, CPM or PERT, several commonalities exist between them. First, all significant activities or tasks must be defined for the entire project. Second, the relationships among the activities must be determined. Third, a network diagram is drawn, assigning numbers to the activity nodes and connecting the activities to graphically represent their relationship to each other. Fourth, time and/or cost estimates are assigned to each activity. Fifth, the critical path is identified by calculating the longest path through the network. Finally, the network is used as a tool to monitor and control the project (Render, 1988, p.

627). "Although PERT and CPM are similar in their basic approach, they do differ in the way activity times are estimated" (Render, 1988, p. 627). In the PERT method a probabilistic approach is used and three time estimates are calculated to determine the expected activity duration and its variance. CPM, however, uses a deterministic method to assign activity durations. Using historical data a duration called the normal time is assigned to each activity. This normal time is the amount of time, under normal circumstances, that it should take to complete the task.

In planning a construction project the process begins by simplifying the entire project into units, or activities, which represent individual work phases. At a macroscopic level these units may represent major phases of the project, or at a microscopic level they may embody very small, specific steps in the construction process. The order of these activities represents the logical order of construction. At this point if the project planner is using arrow diagrams to represent the project, an arrow diagram is constructed diagramming the relationships between the many activities (see Figure 12).

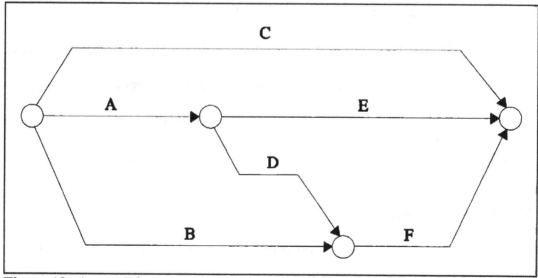

Figure 12 Arrow Diagram

"In order to place the activity arrows of any project in proper sequence, it is necessary to answer three questions for each arrow:

1. What arrows (activities) must precede this one?

2. What arrows (activities) can be concurrent with this one? To be concurrent, activities must start from the same point or finish at the same point.

3. What arrows (activities) must succeed this one?" (Cox, 1986, p. 9).

By answering these three important questions for each activity, the arrow diagram can be constructed, and the relationships among the activities become explicit. In order to allow computerized analysis of the construction schedule, numbered event nodes are implemented. This numbering system, often referred to as an activity's i-j number, thus permits a computer to identify all activities that have a common starting or ending point. The procedure for creating the i-j numbers for the activities is accomplished by beginning with the first activity and assigning numbers to the activity nodes in ascending order. This operation proceeds from left to right skipping an arbitrary number of integers between each node in order to provide space for future expansion of the network. For example, the starting node might be numbered 1, while the next node to the right might be numbered 5. This method proceeds until all activities have a unique i-j number that can later be used to identify individual activities (see Figure 13).

5.2.2 Extension Assumptions

As with all the extensions described so far, certain assumptions must be in place in order to properly frame the context within which these extensions are being

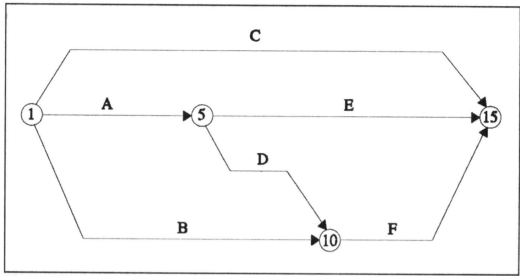

Figure 13 Arrow Diagram with i-j Numbers

created and to limit the scope of the research. For the construction scheduling

extensions, it is important to note that several fundamental and significant differences

exist between the CI-SQL functions that will be detailed next and the features already

available in commercial scheduling packages such as Primavera Project Planner.

First, in the case of commercial packages, there is no industry accepted standard.

Second, the implementation of specific features varies widely from one software

product to the next and may be extremely complex in some cases. Third, many of

the products currently available may be cost prohibitive to many construction

professionals. Conversely, with the implementation of many desirable and industry-

specific functions implemented into SQL, several distinct advantages exist. The

ability to rely upon a widely accepted, world-wide standard for relational query

languages is comforting at least. Also, the implementation of these functions follows

strict guidelines already existing within SQL. Lastly, most companies who use

relational data base technology already own a product that will support SQL queries.

Based on these distinctions, the following assumptions are provided:

1) The intent of adding scheduling functions to SQL is not to replace commercial scheduling packages but rather to provide industry-specific facilities, in a way that has never been done before, to the eminent relational query language.

2) It is acknowledged that many other features are both possible and may be desirable and warrant further research.

3) This work represents a conceptual model upon which full-featured products could be developed.

4) All examples, unless otherwise noted, are based upon the PERT system of project management.

With these assumptions in place, the following sections describe the functions, their syntax, and demonstrate sample queries.

5.2.3 General Scheduling Data Base Structure

Although not nearly as complex as the construction materials data base described earlier, a data base that would properly manage project scheduling data has several important features. First, each activity would be required to have a name or number that could uniquely identify it. In strict relational terms the activity_name column would be the primary key for this data base. Two additional columns, i# and j# would contain the i-j number of each activity. The second and third columns would thus characterize the relationships among activities. At this point, depending on whether the data base were intended to support CPM or PERT, the design would follow one of two paths. In instances where CPM was being used to manage the project a fourth column, duration would hold the value for the estimated time for completion of that activity. Since CPM is a deterministic approach to project scheduling, this duration probably would come from a company's historical data. For PERT projects, however, which is a probabilistic method, the fourth, fifth, and sixth columns would be slightly different. The fourth column, T_o, would receive the optimistic time estimate, or the time an activity will take to complete if everything goes as well as possible. Because this value is based on near perfect conditions, the probability that the activity would be completed in this amount of time should be very small. The fifth column, T_m would contain the most likely time estimate, or the most realistic time to complete the activity. The probability associated with this column's value should be high since this is the most likely time for completion of an activity. The sixth column, T_p, would hold the pessimistic time estimate, that is, the time an activity would take given very unfavorable conditions. The probability associated with this value, like the optimistic time should be very small. This data base layout is illustrated in Figure 14. By no means does this example cover all information applicable to a construction scheduling data base. However, it does provide the necessary basis for the development of the construction-specific extensions to SQL that will be enumerated in subsequent sections.

5.2.4 *concurrent_activities*

The first SQL extension created for construction project scheduling is the *concurrent_activities* function that would retrieve all project activities that occur concurrently with the given activity. To be considered concurrent, activities must start at the same point or finish at the same point. The practical application of this function is obvious. In any construction project it is of critical importance to know the status of any given activity as it relates to the other project tasks. This function

Activity_name	i#	j#	T_o	T_m	T_p
layout_and_excavate	1	3	4	5	6
prefab_forms	1	5	1	3	4
prefab_rebar	1	7	2	3	4
fine_grade	3	5	2	4	5
set_forms	5	7	1	2	4
obtain_backhoe	3	11	1	1	1
set_rebar	7	9	2	3	4
place_concrete	9	11	3	4	6

Figure 14 Construction Scheduling Data Base Layout

provides the user with all activities that commenced at the same time as the activity in question. For example, if the project manager wanted to determine, for coordinating site access, if the crane operator and the concrete pumper would be arriving on the same day, he could retrieve all records that begin at the same time the crane operator arrives. The following syntax extension shows how this function is defined by using the activity name in question as the parameter or argument for the function and returning the concurrent activity or activities.

Syntax:

concurrent_activities ::=

ACTOR FUNCTION *concurrent_activities* (activity_name)

RETURNS activity or activities;

     RETURN SELECT activity_name, i#, j#, duration

FROM Project

WHERE i# = activity_name.i#

OR j# = activity_name.j#

END FUNCTION

Sample Query:

Given a project data base, P1, list all activities that are concurrent with the activity plumbing_rough_in.

Query Form:

SELECT *

FROM P1

WHERE *concurrent_activities* (plumbing_rough_in)

Query Result:

Activity_name	I#	J#	Duration
plumbing_rough_in	8	11	6
fine_grading	8	9	3
lumber_delivery	10	11	1

5.2.5 *preceding_activities*

The second CI-SQL function created for retrieving construction scheduling information is the *preceding_activities* function. This function will retrieve all activities that precede a given activity. For an activity to precede a given activity means that it must end before the given activity can begin. Again, the application of this function is readily apparent. Suppose that a project manager wanted a list of all activities that had to be completed before the brick mason could begin laying the brick veneer for the front of an office complex. The *preceding_activities* function would provide the manager with this information. The syntax extension given below shows how this function is defined by using the activity name in question as the argument for *preceding_activities* and returning the preceding activity or activities.

Syntax:

preceding_activities ::=

ACTOR FUNCTION *preceding_activities* (activity_name)

RETURNS activity or activities;

     RETURN SELECT activity_name, i#, j#, duration

        FROM Project

        WHERE j# = activity_name.i#

     END FUNCTION

Sample Query:

     Given a project data base, P1, list all activities that precede the activity test_electrical_system.

Query Form:

     SELECT *

     FROM P1

     WHERE *preceding_activities* (test_electrical_system)

Query Result:

Activity_name	I#	J#	Duration
test_electrical_system	15	18	1
electrical_rough_in	13	15	11
temp_service_hookup	11	15	1

5.2.6 *succeeding_activities*

The *succeeding_activities* function is designed to retrieve all activities that follow a given activity. If activity 2 succeeds activity 1, activity 2 cannot begin until the completion of activity 1. The *succeeding_activities* function is best illustrated through its use in determining which project activities dictate the commencement of a particular task. For example, if the construction manager desired to see all activities that could not begin until the plumbing subcontractor completed his work, he could retrieve all activities that succeed the plumbing operation. The following example illustrates the use of this function.

Syntax:

succeeding_activities ::=

ACTOR FUNCTION *succeeding_activities* (activity_name)

RETURNS activity or activities;

    RETURN SELECT activity_name, i#, j#, duration

       FROM Project

       WHERE i# = activity_name.j#

    END FUNCTION

Sample Query:

Given a project data base, P1, list all activities that are dependent upon the completion of the drywall crew's work in order to begin.

Query Form:

SELECT *

FROM P1

WHERE *succeeding_activities* (hang_and_finish_drywall)

Query Result:

Activity_name	I#	J#	Duration
hang_and_finish_drywall	22	26	10
hang_wallpaper	26	27	3
paint_drywall	26	30	5

5.2.7 T_e

As mentioned earlier, the PERT scheduling system utilizes probabilities to determine the expected durations of activities. Although this process is straightforward, there is currently no provision for such calculations in SQL. Therefore, this function, T_e will add this desired functionality to the CI-SQL vocabulary. The basic premise behind the PERT method of determining activity durations is that activity duration estimates will follow a beta probability distribution. Using this assumption an expected completion time and variance are calculated for each activity. To find the expected time, T_e, for an activity, the following beta distribution formula is used:

$$\text{Expected Time} = T_e = [(a + 4m + b)/6]^2$$

where $a = T_o = $ optimistic time

m $= T_m = $ most likely time

and $b = T_p = $ pessimistic time.

By adding the functionality of this formula to the builtin capabilities of CI-SQL an activity's expected time for completion can be determined. The implementation of this function, however, is somewhat different from previous functions. The T_e function is implemented similarly to the aggregate functions such as SUM, MIN, and MAX already provided in SQL, in that it is placed in the SELECT clause. However, unlike aggregate functions, which are applied to an entire column and return a single value, the T_e function's argument can be a single activity. Therefore, this function can be grouped with an individual value column without GROUPing on that column. At first this functionality might appear to violate the SQL rule that aggregate functions and individual value columns cannot be mixed in the SELECT clause. However, it is important to remember that this function is not actually an aggregate function since it does not return a single value from an entire column of values. The reason for this is obvious, in that, attempting to find T_e for an entire column would not only be illogical but would not be possible because the argument for this function is a tuple rather than a column. The ensuing explanation shows how this function calculates an activity's expected completion time when passed the parameter activity_name.

Syntax:

$T_e ::=$

ACTOR FUNCTION T_e (activity)

RETURNS T_e;

    RETURN SELECT activity_name, T_e (activity_name)

      FROM Project

        WHERE activity_name = activity_name

    END FUNCTION

The T_e function would be internally defined as:

$$T_e = [\text{activity\_name}.T_o + (4*\text{activity\_name}.T_m) + \text{activity\_name}.T_p]/6$$

in the same way that the AVG, MIN, and MAX functions are currently internally defined for SQL.

Sample Query:

    Given a project data base, P1, calculate the expected time for the activity pour_foundations.

Query Form:

    SELECT T_e(pour_foundations)

    FROM P1

Query Result:

Activity_name	T_e
pour_foundations	5

5.2.8 V

In addition to determining the expected time an activity will take to complete, part of the PERT process is determining the variance of each activity. The dispersion or variance of an activity's time estimate is calculated as:

$$\text{Variance} = V = [(b - a)/6]^2$$

where $\quad$ b = T_p = pessimistic time.

and $\quad$ a = T_o = optimistic time

By providing this capability as an internally defined CI-SQL function, an activity's variance can be calculated.

Like the T_e function the variance function also behaves much like an aggregate function in that it too is placed in the select clause since it calculates a value that may not be explicitly contained in the data base. Since it is not summing or averaging all the values in a given column, this function is not bound by the same constraints as a true aggregate function. The explanation that follows develops the syntax and implementation of the variance function.

Syntax:

$V ::=$

ACTOR FUNCTION V (activity)

RETURNS V;

$\quad$ RETURN SELECT activity_name, V (activity_name)

$\quad\quad$ FROM Project

$\quad\quad$ WHERE activity_name = activity_name

$\quad$ END FUNCTION

The V function would be internally defined as:

$$V = [(\text{activity\_name}.T_p - \text{activity\_name}.T_o)/6]^2$$

in the same way that the AVG, MIN, and MAX functions are currently internally defined for SQL.

Sample Query:

Given a project data base, P1, calculate the variance for the activity excavate_foundations.

Query Form:

SELECT V(excavate_foundations)

FROM P1

Query Result:

Activity_name	V
excavate_foundations	0.11

5.3 Summary

This chapter has set forth the specific content of several crucial extensions to the powerful relational query language, SQL. Two fundamental areas of construction information management have been addressed. Extensions directed at both the selection of construction materials and the retrieval of scheduling information have been created. In both cases the intent of the research has been to develop the process as much as the product. Additionally, a more comprehensive example demonstrating the use of CI-SQL queries has been provided. Although these are not the only SQL functions that can and should be developed for the construction industry, the work represented in this chapter begins an entirely new process in construction research.

CHAPTER 6
CONCLUSIONS

This chapter will summarize the dissertation and its results. Included in this summary will be a synopsis of the CI-SQL functions that have been created to enhance the information management capabilities of the construction industry. Impediments and problems that were encountered in the design process will be addressed, as well as the insights gained in the extension procedure. An examination of future research possibilities and further extensions in construction industry usage will conclude the chapter.

6.1 Summary of Dissertation

The goal of extending ANSI's Structured Query Language necessitated a review of the history and background of SQL. E.F. Codd's contributions in this area were particularly important in that he has set the stage for over twenty years of relational query language development. Although not without criticism, his principles, embodied in the relational model have withstood examination and scrutiny from all angles. It is this solid foundation upon which SQL was designed. Having become an industry standard, SQL has continued to mature through the correction of some of its weaknesses and proposed improvements such as the addition of object data types.

To provide a clear understanding of the basic principles and structure of SQL, a review of its primary functions and syntax was presented. SQL's relational operators, its keys and keywords provided the basis for further development in Chapter 4. Although previous extensions to SQL have been undertaken, none has addressed the unique needs and vernacular of the construction industry. Chapter 4 focused on these distinct requirements and discussed the use of object data typing, object attributes, and user-defined functions as they related to the CI-SQL extensions. After developing the syntax conventions to be utilized in the extensions, two primary domains were examined. In the construction materials domain, five extensions were created that directly confront the selection of materials during the design and bidding phases of the construction process. In the second domain, construction scheduling, an additional five extensions were developed that are applicable to the retrieval of scheduling information. By providing a model for the evolution of construction industry-specific SQL extensions in these two domains, the application of computers for managing construction information has been advanced.

6.2 Results

The primary results of this research are twofold. First, several specific extensions were created which afford the potential for the development of many other related functions. This expansion clearly could be cultivated into a robust collection of construction applications. Second, the development process itself entailed difficulties that yielded unanticipated results. It is the combination of these two types of results that is the true product of this research endeavor.

6.2.1 Functions Created

In all, ten new CI-SQL functions were created from this research. Five of these functions are in the domain of construction materials, and five can be utilized in construction scheduling. The following is a list of those functions with a brief description of each:

1) *complies_with_standard* - retrieves all standards to which a particular product conforms

2) *material_complies_with* - returns a list of materials that meet a given standard

3) *tested_per_test* - determines whether a specified product has been tested against a given test

4) *material_tested_per* - returns the material or materials that have passed a particular test

5) *meets_or_exceeds* - retrieves all products whose specified attribute is greater than or equal to the specified value

6) *concurrent_activities* - retrieves all project activities that occur concurrently with the given activity

7) *preceding_activities* - retrieves all activities that precede a given activity

8) *succeeding_activities* - retrieves all activities that follow a given activity

9) T_e - determines the expected duration of an activity based upon three estimates of its duration

10) V - calculates the statistical variance of a given activity

These functions provide the basis for the development of a comprehensive CI-SQL that could address all the query needs of a complete construction data base. As SQL3 enters the data base environment many other desirable features can be incorporated into CI-SQL that will provide additional benefits to the construction industry in the form of increased efficiency and productivity.

6.2.2 Impediments and Problems

The primary difficulty encountered in developing construction-specific extensions to SQL was remaining within the confines of the SQL construct. Because SQL is not a true programming language many of the facilities commonly available in fourth-generation languages (4GL) are not present in SQL. This statement is not so much a criticism as it is merely a statement of fact. This truth translated into some difficulty in designing features that are easily obtainable in a 4GL, but have not been implemented in SQL. The key circumstance in that this occurred was the attempt to establish extensions that made use of date/time functions. In order to fully provide construction-specific SQL extensions in the area of project scheduling, the ability for SQL to handle date/time math is mandatory. At present SQL provides no such facility. For this reason it is important to address the issue of date/time support necessary for many desired extensions. Based on C.J. Date's work on defining data types, several interdependent steps are necessary to provide adequate support for this function. Initially, the concept of an interval should be defined such that an interval can be added to a date in order to arrive at a future date. In order to perform mathematical operations on intervals, however, conversions must be made between the character format, which humans use to represent dates, and a format that the computer can manipulate. Date suggests that several built-in conversion functions should be created to perform these operations. He describes the following as being desirable:

1) INTERVAL_TO_CHAR and CHAR_TO INTERVAL - These functions would "convert a specified interval to some standard external representation of an interval (e.g., a character string of the form *d:h:m:s*, with a leading minus sign if the interval is negative), and vice versa" (Date, 1990, p. 66), where *d* represents days, *h* hours, *m* minutes, and *s* seconds. As in all of Date's recommended functions, the representation would only need to contain the level of detail desired by the user. For example, in construction scheduling most projects are not scheduled to include hours, minutes, and seconds. Therefore, these values would be either truncated or assigned zeros as placeholders.

2) DATE_TO_CHAR and CHAR_TO_DATE - These functions would convert a conventional calendar date to a form such as *y:n:d:h:m:s* that represents years, months, days, hours, minutes, and seconds respectively. The reverse of this function could also be performed, converting a *y:n:d:h:m:s* representation to a date.

3) INTERVAL_TO_NUM and NUM_TO_INTERVAL - These functions would convert intervals to numbers, and vice versa, with NUM representing the number of specified time units in the given interval.

4) DAY_OF_WEEK - This function would provide the ability to convert a given interval to a number representing the day of the week, where 1 = Sunday, 2 = Monday, etc.

5) DAY_OF_YEAR - This function would provide the ability to convert a given interval to a number representing the day of the year with acceptable values being between 1 and 366.

6) WEEK_OF_YEAR - This function would provide the ability to convert a given interval to a number representing the week of the year with acceptable values being between 1 and 52.

In addition to providing built-in conversion functions, the standard comparisons (<, >, =, <=, >=, and <>) and mathematical operators (+, -, *, and /) would also be supported. The use of the mathematical operators would allow such operations as the addition of two intervals to obtain a third interval, the subtraction of two intervals to obtain a third interval, and the multiplication of an interval by an integer to obtain a new interval. Based on Date's recommendations all the following would be valid date/time expressions under his suggested extensions.

```
SELECT *
FROM Emp
WHERE review_date < CHAR_TO_DATE (:date_parameter);
```

```
SELECT MIN (birth_date)
FROM Emp;
```

```
UPDATE Emp
SET review_date = ADD_MONTHS (review_date, 8)
WHERE Emp# = '1254';
```

Although SQL currently does not support such functionality, according to GE's Donald Deutsch, chairman of ANSI's X3H2 data base committee, similar capabilities will be available in the soon to be released SQL2. When this revision becomes available CI-SQL will be further expandable to encompass many scheduling functions that cannot be accomplished without full-featured date/time capabilities.

6.3 Implications

Since this research focused as much on a process as it did a product, the implications of the research are open-ended. Viewed in a positive way, this provides many opportunities for the future expansion of SQL into almost any industry-specific application. As quickly as SQL is being modified CI-SQL is clearly open for further extensions.

6.3.1 Future Research

This research should be viewed as the first of multiple passes necessary to create a complete and full-featured construction-specific superset of SQL. One of the additional passes necessary to providing a complete version of CI-SQL would be the expansion of construction-specific vocabulary. The development of many other pertinent construction vocabulary words could be achieved through the creation of a consortium of design professionals, construction management personnel, and construction materials experts. The goals of such a consortium should be aimed at developing all vocabulary that would increase productivity by eliminating much of the duplicate effort mentioned earlier. By continuing the process initiated by this research, the tools available for meeting the informational needs of construction professionals can be greatly enhanced. Given the fact that other industries have proprietary vocabularies, the procedure used in this research could be replicated in almost any other industry. Each time a new revision of SQL is released, incorporating additional functions and desired features, CI-SQL and other industry-specific extensions can be taken through another iteration of development. The short time span that apparently will exist between the publication of SQL2 and SQL3 means that it is possible for industry-specific development to experience a similar acceleration.

6.3.2 Future Construction Use

Clearly, future construction use will depend on the future research and release of SQL products. For example, once date/time functions are supported by SQL, construction applications such as calculating expected material delivery dates will be feasible. Also, many scheduling operations such as calculating activity float times, and projected project completion dates will be possible. Other construction activities such as cost estimating and bid analysis should be examined for applicable uses and extensions of SQL.

In addition to building CI-SQL based on future research, extensive data base development would be required in order to provide the construction industry with critical data such as pricing and availability of products. The development of such data bases would depend largely upon the participation of manufacturing groups to furnish detailed product information. This information would have to include attribute templates, or models of all the data that uniquely identify individual products or groups of products. For example, the attribute template for doors might include such fields as size, swing, thickness, material, lites, style, and fire rating. Characteristics such as these would allow an architect or contractor to specify the values for each of these attributes that uniquely identify doors. Thus, participation on the part of manufacturers would be crucial to the success of building large construction materials data bases that could be used by the construction industry to increase productivity.

APPENDIX A
ACTUAL PROJECT SPECIFICATIONS

Note: Construction vocabulary is indicated by boldface type.

Example 1
SECTION 08110
STEEL DOORS AND FRAMES

PART 1 - GENERAL

1.1 DESCRIPTION OF WORK

    A.   Finish Hardware: Refer to Section 80710.
    B.   Painting: Refer to Section 09900.
      1. Colors: Refer to Section 09000.

1.2 QUALITY ASSURANCE:

A. Provide doors and frames **complying with** Steel Door Institute Recommended Specifications: Standard Steel Doors and Frames" (SDI-100) and as herein specified.
  1. Fire-Rated Door Assemblies: Where fire-rated door assemblies are indicated or required, provide fire-rated door and frame assemblies that **comply with** NFPA 80 "Standard for Fire Doors and Windows", and have been tested, listed, and labeled in accordance with ASTM E 152 "Standard Methods of Fire Tests of Door Assemblies" by a nationally recognized independent testing and inspection agency acceptable to authorities having jurisdiction.

1.2 SUBMITTALS:

A. Product Data: Submit seven (7) copies of manufacturer's technical product data substantiating that products **comply with** requirements.
B. Shop Drawings: Submit seven (7) copies of fabrication and installation of steel doors and frames. Include details of each frame type, elevations of door design types, conditions at openings, details of construction, location and installation requirements of finish hardware and reinforcements, and details of joints and connections. Show anchorage and accessory items.
  1. Provide schedule of doors and frames using same reference numbers for details and opening as those on contract drawings.

1.3 DELIVERY, STORAGE AND HANDLING:

A. Deliver hollow metal work cartoned or crated to provide protection during transit and job storage. Provide additional sealed plastic wrapping for factory finished doors.

B. Inspect hollow metal work upon delivery for damage. Minor damages may be repaired provided finish items are equal in all respects to new work and acceptable to the Architect; otherwise, remove and replace damaged items as directed.

C. Store doors and frames at building site under cover and protect from damage.

PART 2 - PRODUCTS

2.1 ACCEPTABLE MANUFACTURERS:

A. Manufacturers: Subject to compliance with requirements, manufacturers offering steel doors and frames which may be incorporated in the work include, but are not limited to, the following:

1. Allied Steel Products, Inc.
2. Ceco corporation
3. Republic Builders Prod. Corporation
4. Firedoor Corporation of Florida.

2.2 MATERIALS:

A. Hot-Rolled Steel sheets and Strip: Commercial Quality carbon steel, pickled and oiled, **complying with ASTM A 569 and ASTM A 568.**

B. Cold-Rolled Steel Sheets: Commercial quality carbon steel, **complying with** ASTM A 366 and ASTM A 568.

C. Galvanized Steel Sheets: Zinc-coated carbon steel sheets of commercial quality, **complying with** ASTM A 526, with ASTM A 525, G60 zinc coating, mill phosphatized.

Example 2

SECTION 15001

2.3 MOTORS

A. Refer to the equipment schedules and specification sections for specific voltages required.

B. All motors shall be 1750 RPM, unless otherwise noted.

C. Use NEMA Design B motors, normal starting torque with Class B insulation unless specified otherwise or unless the manufacturer of the equipment on which the motor is being used has different requirements. All motors to have a 1.15 service factor.

D. All motors 1 HP and larger, except specially wound motors, shall be high efficiency design. Nominal efficiency of each high efficiency motor **shall meet or exceed** the value listed below when tested in accordance with NEMA MG 1-12.53a and 1-12.53b.

HP	1200 rpm	1800 rpm	3600 rpm
1	81	82	80
1 1/2	84	82	81
2	84	84	82
3	86	85	82
5	87	87	85
7 1/2	89	88	87
10	89	89	88
15	90	91	89
20	91	91	91
25	91	92	91
30	91	92	91
40	91	92	91
50	91	92	91

E. All equipment furnished under this contract utilizing a combined electrical load of greater than 100 Watts shall have a power factor of not less than .85 under rated load condition.

1. Where motors are not available with minimum .85 power factor, provide motor mounted power factor correction capacitor to improve power factor to at least .90 under rated load condition.

F. Single phase motors for hard starting applications including outdoor applications single phase operation shall be capacitor start type, motors for hard starting applications including outdoor applications. Motors for fans and pumps located indoor may be split phase or permanent split-capacitor. Motors shall be equipped with permanently lubricated and sealed ball bearings, and shall be selected for quiet operation. Motors 1/8 HP and below may be shaded pole type with permanently oiled unit bearings.

G. Unless otherwise indicated, two speed motors to be one winding, consequent pole, variable torque type.

Part 3 - EXECUTION

3.1   INSTALLATION

A.   Install materials in accordance with details, approved shop drawings, and manufacturers' instructions.

END OF SECTION 15001

APPENDIX B
CSI MASTERSPEC FORMAT

Division 01 GENERAL REQUIREMENTS

Division 02 SITE WORK

Division 03 CONCRETE

Division 04 MASONRY

Division 05 METALS

Division 06 WOOD & PLASTICS

Division 07 THERMAL & MOISTURE PROTECTION

Division 08 DOORS & WINDOWS

Division 09 FINISHES

Division 10 SPECIALTIES

Division 11 EQUIPMENT

Division 12 FURNISHINGS

Division 13 SPECIAL CONSTRUCTION

Division 14 CONVEYING SYSTEMS

Division 15 MECHANICAL

Division 16 ELECTRICAL

SAMPLE SCREENS FROM SWEET'S SWEETSEARCH ON CD-ROM

Note: Selection choices are shown in boldface type.

SweetSearch
Building Product Search Systems

SweetSearch can lead you to products in Sweet's Catalog Files in a number of ways. Use Keyword Search to find products using familiar words or phrases. Use Product Search to find products with specific characteristics. Choose Manufacturer Search to review products of a selected manufacturer. Trade Name Search displays products bearing a given Trade Name, while the Catalog Search brings up all products in a specific catalog. Association/Agency Search shows what information is available from the Association selected. If this is your first use of SweetSearch, press F1 for help.

Select #1

      1-Keyword Search
      2-Product Search
      3-Manufacturer Search
      4-Trade Name Search
      5-Catalog Search
      6-Association/Agency Search
      7-Set-up

F1Help F2RestoreMark EscExit

PRODUCT: In SweetSearch, as in the Sweet's Catalog Files, all product types are grouped into the standard 16 divisions. Select the division wanted by using the arrow keys or typing the list number, then press Enter.

Select #1

1 General Data	9 Finishes
2 Sitework	10 Specialties
3 Concrete	11 Equipment
4 Masonry	12 Furnishings
5 Metals	13 Special Construction
6 Wood and Plastics	14 Conveying Systems
7 Thermal & Moisture Protection	15 Mechanical
8 Doors & Windows	16 Electrical

F1Help F10MainMenu EscGoBack

PRODUCT: The classification sections for this division are the same as those listed in Sweet's Catalog Files. Select the classification section by using the arrow keys or typing the list number, then press Enter.

Select # 1

1 08100-Metal Doors And Frames	18 08385-Sound Control Doors
2 08200-Wood and Plastic Doors	19 08390-Screen & Storm Doors
3 08275-Door Louvers/Vision Lights	20 08400-Entrances & Storefronts
4 08300-Special Doors	21 08455-Fire Res Glass Wl&Door Asmbly
5 08305-Access Doors	22 08470-Revolving Entrance Doors
6 08315-Blast-Resistant Doors	23 08500-Metal Windows
7 08316-Air & Watertight Doors	24 08610-Wood Windows
8 08320-Detention/Security Doors	25 08630-Plastic Windows
9 08325-Cold Storage Doors	26 08640-Glazed Patio Doors
10 08330-Coiling Doors & Grilles	27 08652-Replacement Windows
11 08350-Folding Doors & Grilles	28 08653-Sound Control Windows
12 08352-Folding Fire Barriers	29 08660-Detention/Secur Wnds & Screens
13 08360-Upward Acting Sect. Doors	30 08665-Pass and Observation Windows
14 08370-Industrial & Hangar Doors	31 08667-Ext Roll-Up Window Shutters
15 08375-Hangar Doors	32 08668-Ext Folding, Sliding Shutters
16 08380-Traffic/Impact Doors	33 08670-Storm Sash & Screens
17 08382-Darkroom Doors	34 08710-Finish Hardware

List Continues PgDn For More

F1Help F10MainMenu EscGoBack

PRODUCT: The classification sections for this division are the same as those listed in Sweet's Catalog Files. Select the classification section by using the arrow keys or typing the list number, then press Enter.

Select # 35

35 08716-Exit Devices
36 08718-Sld/Folding Door Hardware
37 08720-Operators
38 08730-Weatherstripping/Thresholds
39 08760-Window Hardware & Special
40 08780-Cabinet & Drawer Hardware
41 08810-Glass

42 08820-Decorative Glazing
43 08840-Plastic Glazing
44 08850-Glazing & Glass Block Accs
45 08870-Glazing Film
46 08900-Glazed Curtain Walls
47 08950-Translucent Wall Systems
48 08960-Sloped Glazing Systems

List Complete Use PgUp

F1Help F10MainMenu EscGoBack

PRODUCT: Several types of products are included in this section. Make your selection, then press ENTER to begin your search.

Select # 1

1 08200/1-Wood & Plastic Doors
2 08200/2-Wood Frames

PRODUCT: Each criterion will bring up a set of detail selection characteristics. Choose your most important criteria, via arrow keys or the list number, then press Enter. For a listing of appropriate manufacturers, press F5.

Select # 1   WOOD & PLASTIC DOORS   Product Count 243

1 -Type/Design: MATERIAL
2 -Assemblies/Combinations: 12-Flush Door: Face Panel:
3 -Specific Application: 13-Flush Door: Core:
4 -Special Properties: 14-Stile & Rail Doors:
5 -Grade Per AWI: 15-Factory Finishes:
6 -Features:
7 -Options/Accessories: PERFORMANCE CHARACTERISTICS
8 -Lites: 16-Fire Resistance:
9 -Louvers: 17-Thermal Transmittance:
10-Standard Size Range: 18-Snd Transmission Class:
11-Custom Fabrication: 19-Conformance:

F1Help F3Undo F5Mfr F7Clear F8Tutorial F9Print F10MainMenu EscGoBack

APPENDIX D
GLOSSARY OF TERMS

Aggregate Function - A group function; a function operating on the values in one column of a table and producing a single value as its result.

Attributes - A named characteristic or property of an entity.

Base Table - Any "real" table in the data base, as opposed to a "virtual" table.

Boolean Expression - An expression which returns either true or false as its result.

Cardinality - The number of rows in a given table.

Character Strings - A sequence of characters.

Data Control Language - (DCL) - One category of SQL statements; these statements control access to the data and to the data base and include: GRANT CONNECT, GRANT SELECT, UPDATE ON, and REVOKE DBA.

Data Definition Language (DDL) - The language component of a DBMS that is used to describe the logical (and sometimes physical) structure of a data base.

Data Manipulation Language (DML) - A language component of a DBMS that is used by a programmer to access and modify the contents of a data base.

Data Base - A shared collection of logically related data, designed to meet the information needs of multiple users.

Degree - The number of columns in a given table.

Duplicate Row - A record or tuple or row in a data base containing the same data as another row in the same table.

Entity - A person, place, object, or concept about which an organization chooses to store data.

Entity-Relationship Model - A type of network data model that uses a special symbol (the diamond) to represent associations between entities.

Field - A part of a table that holds one piece of data; the intersection of a row and a column.

Four-Valued Logic - In addition to providing the support that three-valued logic does, four-valued logic also supports "not-applicable" as a valid result of a comparison.

Fourth-Generation Language (4GL) - A high-level non-procedural language that allows users to write programs much faster than with COBOL or other third-generation languages.

Gateway - The computer or software used to provide access between different data bases.

Identity - The property which distinguishes an object from any other object.

Information Object - A time-dependent collection of information which may often be use to model some object outside the data base, such as a person or a plan.

Inheritance - The ability of an information object to inherit the attributes and operations of another object, typically on in its superclass.

Instance - An occurrence of an entity or a data type. For example, a personnel record is a record type; the record for Sally Jones is an instance of that record type.

Integrity - Refers to the accuracy, validity, or correctness of the data in the data base.

Key - An attribute or data item that uniquely identifies a record instance or tuple in a relation.

Nesting - An arrangement of two processing steps in which one invokes the other.

Normalization - The process of decomposing complex data structures into simple relations according to a set of dependency rules.

ODBMS - Object Data Base Management System; the support facilities provided through software for managing the data in an object-oriented data base.

Predicate Clause - A clause based on one of the operators (=, !=, IS, IS NOT, >, >=, <, <=) and containing no AND, OR, or NOT.

Procedural Language - A programming language that requires programming discipline, such as COBOL, FORTRAN, BASIC and C.

Programming Language - A language used to write instructions for the computer.

RDBMS - Relational Data Base Management System; the set of tools provided by a data base system for managing relational data.

Relational Operators - Relational operators allow the performance of basic set processing on tables.

Relational Model - A logical data model in which all data are represented as a collection of normalized relations.

SQL - Structured Query Language. A standard data definition and manipulation language for relational data bases.

SQL Engine - A program that accepts an SQL command and accesses the database to obtain the requested data.

SQL Server - A database engine from Sybase, Inc., that runs on IBM compatible file servers and uses the SQL language as its primary interface.

Structure - The format or design of a data base.

Three-Valued Logic - A three-valued logic system is one in which any comparison will always result in a "true", "false", or "null" value.

Tuple - A row in a table or relation.

View - A table that does not physically exist as such in storage, but looks to the user as though it does; a part of a table that does exist in the data base; a virtual table.

Virtual Table - A table that does not actually exist in the data base but looks to the user as though it does.

REFERENCES

Antill, J.M., & Woodhead, R.W. (1970). <u>Critical path methods in construction practice</u>. New York: Wiley-Interscience.

Beech, D. (1989a, February 1). New life for SQL. <u>Datamation</u>, pp. 29-36.

Beech, D. (1989b, February 15). The future of SQL. <u>Datamation</u>, pp. 45-48.

Beech, D., & Ozbutun, C. (1991). Object data bases as generalizations of relational data bases. <u>Computer Standards & Interfaces, 13</u>, 221-230.

Busch, D.H. (1991). <u>The new critical path method</u>. Chicago: Probus Publishing Company.

Codd, E.F. (1970). A relational model of data for large shared data banks. <u>Communications of the ACM</u>, 13(6), 377-387

Codd, E.F. (1988a, August 15). Fatal flaws in SQL. <u>Datamation</u>, pp. 45-48.

Codd, E.F. (1988b, September 1). Fatal flaws in SQL. <u>Datamation</u>, pp. 71-74.

Cox, R. (1986). <u>CPM scheduling for the construction contractor</u>. Gainesville, FL: Author.

Crutchfield, R. J. (1990, Fall). Data to the desktop: The SQL advantage. <u>Byte</u>, pp. 193-198.

Date, C.J. (1988a). Defining data types in a data base language. <u>ACM SIGMOD Record</u>, 17(2), 12-23.

Date, C.J. (1988b). Why relational? <u>The Relational Journal</u>, 3(4), 38-52.

Date, C.J. (1989). <u>A guide to the SQL standard</u> (2nd ed.). Reading, MA: Addison-Wesley Publishing Company.

Date, C.J. (1990). <u>Relational data base writings 1985-1989</u>. Reading, MA: Addison-Wesley Publishing Company.

Date, C.J., & White, C. J. (1989). <u>A guide to SQL/DS</u>. Reading, MA: Addison-Wesley Publishing Company.

Egenhofer, M. J. (1989). Spatial query languages. Dissertation Abstracts International, 51, 5104A. (University Microfilms No. 9023850)

Faulkner, E. (1973). Project management with CPM. Duxbury, MA: R.S. Means Co., Inc.

Glass, B. (1991, March 11). Data base tower of babel: Portable SQL still a dream. Infoworld, p. S14.

Hursch, C. J., & Hursch, J. L. (1988). SQL: The structured query language. Blue Ridge Summit, PA: Tab Books Inc.

Jones, R. (1989). SQL--Problems with an emerging standard. Information and Software Technology, 31(1), 2-6.

Martyn, T., & Hartley, T. (1989). DB2/SQL: A professional programmer's guide. New York: McGraw-Hill Book Company.

McFadden, F. R., & Hoffer, J. A. (1988). Data base management. Menlo Park, CA: Benjamin/Cummings Publishing Company, Inc.

Miller, R. (1963). Schedule, cost, and profit control with PERT. New York: McGraw-Hill Book Company.

Mitrani, J.D. (1977). The critical path method: A self-study text. Gainesville, FL: Construction Bookstore, Inc.

Moad, J. (1990, September 15). The standards process breaks down. Datamation, pp. 24-32.

Pascal, F. (1988a, August 8). Vital stats for DBMS shoppers. Computerworld, p. 33.

Pascal, F. (1988b, August 15). SQL can often be just the ticket for DBMSs. Computerworld, p. 51.

Pascal, F. (1989a, February 27). Misunderstood and maligned, RDBMSs fight a bum rap. Computerworld, pp. 76-77.

Pascal, F. (1989b, September). A brave new world? Byte, pp. 247-256.

Pratt, P. J. (1990). A guide to SQL. Boston: Boyd & Fraser Publishing Company.

Render, B., & Stair, R.M. (1988). Quantitative analysis for management. Boston: Allyn and Bacon Inc.

Sayles, J. S. (1990). Embedded SQL for DB2: Application design and programming. Wesley, MA: QED Information Sciences, Inc.

Sikeler, A. (1985). Examination of storage structures for 3-dimensional objects (Technical Report) Kaiserslautern, West Germany: University Kaiserslautern.

Trimble, J. H., & Chappell, D. (1989). A visual introduction to SQL. New York: John Wiley & Sons.

Van Name, M. L., & Catchings, B. (1989, Fall). SQL: A data base language sequel to Dbase. BYTE, pp. 175-182.

Wipper, F. (1989). Guide to DB2 and SQL/DS. New York: McGraw-Hill Publishing Company.

BIOGRAPHICAL SKETCH

Kevin Cole Hollister was born on August 12, 1965, in Chattanooga, Tennessee. Shortly thereafter, his family moved to Tampa, Florida, where he lived until graduation from Chamberlain High School in 1983. His interest in construction began in 1984 when he took a course titled "Build Your Dream Home." The following year he entered the School of Building Construction at the University of Florida and graduated with a bachelor's degree in the fall of 1987. Upon completion of this degree, he began graduate work in building construction and earned a Master of Science in Building Construction in the fall of 1988. The following semester he entered the College of Architecture's Ph.D. program. His career goals include expanding the use of microcomputers in the construction industry and eventually teaching in Florida's university system.

I certify that I have read this study and that in my opinion it conforms to acceptable standards of scholarly presentation and is fully adequate, in scope and quality, as a dissertation for the degree of Doctor of Philosophy.

Weilin P. Chang, Chair
Professor of Building Construction

I certify that I have read this study and that in my opinion it conforms to acceptable standards of scholarly presentation and is fully adequate, in scope and quality, as a dissertation for the degree of Doctor of Philosophy.

Charles J. Kibert
Associate Professor of Building Construction

I certify that I have read this study and that in my opinion it conforms to acceptable standards of scholarly presentation and is fully adequate, in scope and quality, as a dissertation for the degree of Doctor of Philosophy.

Gary J. Koehler
Professor of Decision and Information Sciences

I certify that I have read this study and that in my opinion it conforms to acceptable standards of scholarly presentation and is fully adequate, in scope and quality, as a dissertation for the degree of Doctor of Philosophy.

Carleton Coulter III
Professor of Building Construction

This dissertation was submitted to the Graduate Faculty of the College of Architecture and to the Graduate School, and was accepted as partial fulfillment of the requirements for the degree of Doctor of Philosophy.

August 1992

R. Wayne Drummond

Dean, College of Architecture

Dean, Graduate School

www.ingramcontent.com/pod-product-compliance
Lightning Source LLC
Chambersburg PA
CBHW080429060326
40689CB00019B/4436